Curriculum Studies as an International Conversation

Examining Curriculum Studies from an international perspective, this book focuses on the relations between the Anglo-Saxon and Latin American educational traditions. Informed by William F. Pinar's conceptualization of curriculum as *currere*, Johnson-Mardones reconsiders curriculum as an international conversation and advances an intercultural dialogue among educational traditions to put forth a more comprehensive and inclusive theory of curriculum. Moving beyond the Anglo-Saxon space and into the Global South, Johnson-Mardones brings in his own non-Western educational experience to the center of this inquiry, and situates cosmopolitanism as a necessary but complex component of Curriculum Studies.

Daniel F. Johnson-Mardones is a researcher at University of Chile, Chile.

Studies in Curriculum Theory
William F. Pinar, Series Editor

Curriculum Studies as an International Conversation
Educational Traditions and Cosmopolitanism in Latin America
Johnson-Mardones

Engaging Curriculum
Bridging the Curriculum Theory and English Education Divide
Green

Arts Education and Curriculum Studies
The Contributions of Rita L. Irwin
Carter & Triggs

Sound Curriculum
Sonic Studies in Educational Theory, Method & Practice
Gershon

Place, Race, and Identity Formation
Autobiographical Intersections in a Curriculum Theorist's Daily Life
McKnight

Reconceptualizing Study in Educational Discourse and Practice
Ruitenberg

The Mythopoetics of Currere
Memories, Dreams and Literary Texts as Teaching Avenues to Self-Study
Doll

Christian Privilege in U.S. Education
Legacies and Current Issues
Burke/Segal

For additional information on titles in the Studies in Curriculum Theory series visit www.routledge.com/education

Curriculum Studies as an International Conversation
Educational Traditions and Cosmopolitanism in Latin America

Daniel F. Johnson-Mardones

NEW YORK AND LONDON

First published 2018
by Routledge
711 Third Avenue, New York, NY 10017

and by Routledge
2 Park Square, Milton Park, Abingdon, Oxon, OX14 4RN

Routledge is an imprint of the Taylor & Francis Group, an informa business

© 2018 Taylor & Francis

The right of Daniel F. Johnson-Mardones to be identified as author of this work has been asserted by him in accordance with sections 77 and 78 of the Copyright, Designs and Patents Act 1988.

All rights reserved. No part of this book may be reprinted or reproduced or utilized in any form or by any electronic, mechanical, or other means, now known or hereafter invented, including photocopying and recording, or in any information storage or retrieval system, without permission in writing from the publishers.

Trademark notice: Product or corporate names may be trademarks or registered trademarks, and are used only for identification and explanation without intent to infringe.

Library of Congress Cataloging-in-Publication Data
A catalog record has been requested for this book

ISBN: 978-0-8153-6869-4 (hbk)
ISBN: 978-1-351-25406-9 (ebk)

Typeset in Sabon
by Apex CoVantage, LLC

Contents

1 Introduction: Understanding Curriculum as an
  International Conversation   1

2 A Theoretical *Détente*   26

3 The Regressive-Progressive   41

4 The Analytical-Synthetical   77

5 Conclusion: Cosmopolitanism in a Latin American Key   116

  Index   131

1 Introduction

Understanding Curriculum as an International Conversation

Coming to Profess

There is a personal involvement in the study of every field. Deepened, that study becomes devotion; then, it can be said one professes that field. To me that field is the field of Curriculum Studies. To understand curriculum is to tell the story of our coming into being in that field. It is to draw the sketches that map our academic journey, our coming to profess. In coming to profess, we study those who professed that field before us. We dig in and within a tradition, or more than one. In that endeavor "[w]e must re-define and re-conceptualize" (Dussel, 1976, p. 16) the field. In other words, to study a tradition is to reinvent it. That study certainly transforms us and we transform that tradition. For me, that is the passing on of the intellectual experience of two such creative generations, one from the United States, the other from Latin America.

Listening to those two generations, the one that undertook the reconceptualization of Curriculum Studies in the United States during the 1970s and the one that devoted itself to the creation of an authentic Latin American thinking since the 1960s, I find insights for my own search: an understanding of curriculum as an international conversation. I accept the need for re-definition, for re-conceptualization, for recontextualization of concepts developed in other latitudes and other times. Just as "[e]ach generation must draw its line in the sand and take a stance toward the past" (Denzin & Lincoln, 2011, p. x), I do too. While engaged in that liminal relationality, I take a distance that is historical, geographical, cultural, and generational. I make the Anglo-Saxon American field of curriculum my object of study in order to enable an intergenerational and intercultural dialogue in Curriculum Studies as an international academic field. I understand internationalization as a dialogue among colleagues, a conversation among adults. That, I believe, must be at the front of a field still becoming an international conversation informed by distinct intellectual histories and present circumstances and still in need of becoming historical (Pinar, 2011a). My *locus enuntiationis* remains *Latinoamérica*; in the underside of modernity, it could not be otherwise.

In writing this book, my departure point is my own educational doctoral experience in a Department of Curriculum and Instruction in a public university in the United States. In that experience, the United States and Latin American educational traditions collide in a complicated manner both biographical and historical. Furthermore, for those of us coming from the underside of modernity, in thinking about our professing intellectual disciplines born in the center (e.g., Curriculum Studies) we must question ourselves about the geopolitics involved in the development of those fields and the displacement into which our intellectual curiosity takes us. In other words, while studying those traditions, some of us may want to situate our *locus enuntiationis* in the periphery (Latin America) of the world-system (Wallerstein, 2004)—the place of the *Otro* [Other]—rather than in its center. I believe that is the right move for a generation in an effort to study its legacy without remaining passive receptacles and obsessive repeaters. Our task today is not to uncritically import intellectual traditions, or even new or old critiques, but to engage in dialogue with them, to make our own critique.

Sartre's preface to Fanon's *The Wretched of the Earth* is quite suggestive about this. He writes: "[for] the fathers [a previous generation in the colonies], we [the Europeans] alone were the speakers; the sons [a new generation in the colonies] no longer even consider us as valid intermediaries: we are the objects of their speeches" (In Fanon, 2004, p. 10). The new generation coming out of the process of decolonization does not remain silent. Unlike the previous generation, these newcomers no longer just repeat the Discourses of the center. They are not passive listeners anymore. They also speak and they do it first by making the discourse of the center their object of study. I cannot avoid feeling a certain affinity between my project here and the one that Sartre delineates to introduce Fanon's work. Regardless of the differences in the postcolonial situation in Africa and Asia, *Latinoamérica* in the 1960s had also become aware of having been for centuries named and written from the outside. The project of developing an authentic Latin American thinking became the project of a generation coming to intellectual adulthood in the 1960s. There was the necessity to name *Latinoamérica* by its proper name. Freire wrote within that tradition, the Latin American thinkers of liberation.[1]

When it comes to Curriculum Studies, Freire appears as one of the first Latin Americans to talk back to a neocolonial process that ended up shaping my schooling while growing up in a dictatorship sponsored by the same country that sponsored the import of the field I come now to profess. The field that would become of my educational "given" was the result of the United States' intervention in Chile, and in *Latinoamérica*, in which the arriving of the field of curriculum and the traumatic violence of the Coup d'Etat were part of the same will to power. As I said, this conversation is complicated, both historically and biographically. It is not just an intellectually challenging conversation but, for me, also an emotionally charged one.

Curriculum development became the language of education in Chile from the second half of the 1960s. That language endured during the dictatorship that followed the military takeover in the country in 1973, which also prevented the field of curriculum from intellectual renewal during the decades to come. The two possible sources of renovation for the emerging field were either unknown in the case of outsiders (the authors of the U.S. reconceptualization, for instance), given the country's forced isolation; or censored and in exile, in the case of the insiders (for example, Freire). What remained in Chile, for at least two decades, was a field arrested under the technocratic approach of *curriculum development*. That "given" lasted during the Chilean "transition to democracy" in the 1990s, the time I went to college to become a teacher.

The Latin American tradition, as opposed to curriculum as an educational technology, was also a "given;" one of a different sort, however. It was a "given" that sought its own voice, its being for itself, in Freire's expression. While also a "given," Paulo Freire was yet a distinctive language to name education. A language developed on the outskirts of schooling and society. It was a language of education as a practice of freedom. I read Freire in the 1990s outside of my university's classes, where there was no room for his work in courses dominated by Tyler and his principles, Bloom and his taxonomy, Gagné and his domains, Bruner and his process. Yet I read Freire while at the university, being introduced to his work through my participation in the church and my engagement in the study of liberation theology. He was part of my lived curriculum and much more than that. I did not realize at that time that Freire was talking back to the U.S. tradition of curriculum as imported under the shadow of *curriculum development* and Tyler rationale. I did not make that connection then; I do it now. I did not know that a talking back had also taken place in the United States, with the name of reconceptualization, just a few years after Freire's main writings were published there. In Chile, as in many parts of the world, that process of reconceptualization of the field of curriculum in the United States remained largely unknown. These realizations, I believe, are among the most important points that my doctoral studies have helped me to achieve. They have certainly forged my understanding of curriculum as an international conversation.

Curriculum Studies as an International Conversation

The field of curriculum is embedded within national cultures. Historically, the nation state has been the unit of analysis and prescription in Curriculum Studies. Traditionally, this reality relied on the idea of a selective tradition (Apple, 1979; Weis, McCarthy, & Dimitriadis, 2006; Williams, 1961) worthy to be passed on to the country's next generation.

4 Introduction

This was still the case at the beginning of this century, and today. In tandem, a growing awareness of the increasingly diverse and global world seemed to require that Curriculum Studies needed to incorporate international perspectives (Pinar, 2014c; Popkewitz, 2013; Tröhler, 2011; Yates & Grumet, 2011; Ropo & Autio, 2009; Autio, 2006; Trueit, 2003; Westbury, Hopmann, & Riquarts, 2000). Hence, the nation state could no longer be taken for granted as the exclusive unit for understanding curriculum. Furthermore, internationally, the dominant influence of the United States Curriculum Studies field may not have been as strong as I expected it to be, given that curriculum was a U.S. tradition. The study of this process and its potential has been undertaken under the term *internationalization*.

The term *internationalization*, as well as the worldwide intellectual movement named by it, is deeply connected to the scholarship of William F. Pinar. Explaining his proposal to an international community of scholars in his address to the first *International Conference for the Advancement of Curriculum Studies* at Louisiana State University (LSU) in 2001, Pinar suggested that curriculum theorists should "depict the field's efforts to extend its scholarly conversation beyond the national borders in which it is practiced" (Pinar, 2006, p. 165). The choice of the word internationalization instead of globalization, Pinar explained, rests on the totalizing and standardizing dynamic that the latter entails and that resonates with a neocolonial and neo-imperialistic past. The term internationalization does not carry these associations.

Since then, the literature regarding internationalization has grown. This is increasingly expressed in the publications associated with the *International Association for the Advancement of Curriculum Studies* founded in 2001(IAASC). The main procedures of the conferences maintained by the *International Association for the Advancement of Curriculum Studies* have been published as edited books. Since 2004, the IAASC also publishes its own journal, *The Journal of Transnational Curriculum Inquiry*. The American *Association for the Advancement of Curriculum Studies* (AAACS), affiliated to IAACS, also includes scholarship on internationalization in its annual meetings and in its journal. Another association affiliated to IAACS, the *European Association of Curriculum Studies* (EACS) also publishes on this topic. Furthermore, the EACS is itself an example of the internationalization of Curriculum Studies since the field of curriculum is not a continental field or not as old as others there. Besides these institutional spaces, the two editions of the *International Handbook of Curriculum Research* (Pinar, 2003, 2014c) constitute major contributions for the understanding of curriculum as an international academic field. In its two editions, this handbook includes opening chapters that theorize the process of internationalization, followed by chapters that offer specific regional or national accounts of the field of curriculum worldwide. Another series of publications focuses on specific countries in which William F. Pinar engages curriculum scholars in a dialogue in order to understand the current circumstances and intellectual histories of Curriculum Studies in those national contexts. This international actualization of Pinar's concept of complicated conversation is represented in the publication of edited books on Curriculum Studies in Brazil (Pinar, 2011b), China (Pinar, 2014b), India (Pinar, 2015a), Mexico (2011b), and South Africa (Pinar, 2010). In addition, numerous articles have been published in the main journals in the field, such as *Curriculum Inquiry* and *Journal of Curriculum Studies*, being good examples of the internationalization of the field. *The SAGE Handbook of Curriculum and Instruction* (Connelly, He, & Phillion, 2008), dedicated one of its sections to "Internationalizing Curriculum;" the *Curriculum Studies Handbook: The Next Moment* (Malewski, 2010) dedicates one of its parts to "Cross-Cultural International Perspectives." In addition, *Division B: Curriculum Studies* of the *American Educational Research Association* (AERA) has consistently organized spaces for scholarship discussing internationalization during its annual meetings.

Regarding the field of Curriculum Studies in the United States, curriculum as an international conversation seems to provide the possibility of an intellectual distance from the national context, enabling reconstruction. Through that distancing, Pinar argues, the U.S. curriculum field can emerge from the reconceptualization movement as more cosmopolitan; that is, according to Pinar, the "generative potential of the dislocation of the 'stranger'" (Pinar, 2006, p. 170). According to him, internationalization can provoke reconstruction and creation. That is the role that Pinar's study of the field in Brazil, South Africa, Mexico, China, and India can play in relation to the field in the United States. This idea, if contextualized in the field in the United States, entails the possibility of reconstruction of the field in any national context. Therefore, national accounts of the field, some of them not yet written, may serve as performative texts that trigger someone else's self-reflection. In other words, putting those accounts into a complicated conversation can provoke self-reflective processes and enable new self-narratives in a national context.

The potential of internationalization, nevertheless, is not limited to 'moving beyond the nation' in order to reconstruct the national narrative or to reformulate a national canon; it also includes the exploration of international conversations as in-between scholarly spaces. Authentic international engagement requires that somehow the "very terms of this study become objects of study and not only for those working in North America" (Pinar, 2006, p. 167). Internationalization itself is also one of those terms in need of becoming an object of study especially for those working outside of the United States, where the term was born in Curriculum Studies. I believe curriculum international scholarship requires a new language in Curriculum Studies; "such a language would be one that grows in the middle" (Aoki, 2005, p. 49). That "middle" is the liminal space we dwell in when moving across historical contexts in which we talk curriculum.

Thus, *analectically* (Dussel, 1973, 1980, 1985) inspired, I think of the term internationalization within the context of Curriculum Studies and from the *locus enuntiationis* of my Latin American and global southernness to unfold the international as a dimension of Curriculum Studies that has expressed itself distinctively throughout our recent history. This is also to say that I think about the internationalization of Curriculum Studies through the relationality of the national and the global and its intertwinings in intellectual histories and biographies. From that geopolitical perspective, internationalization has been a dimension of the field of Curriculum Studies. The current internationalization movement can be considered the last wave of internationalization in this field.

Three Waves of Internationalization

Looking from the Global South (De Sousa Santos, 2014), internationalization has always been part of the field of Curriculum Studies since its consolidation in the United States at the end of the 1940s.[2] In fact, in the field of education international initiatives have usually been associated with neocolonial efforts. Usually promoted by international organizations, these perspectives are positioned as educational innovations grounded on so-called international evidence. Thus, the main historical periods suggested by Pinar (2008, 2014a) acquired a new meaning when situated at global scale; I am calling them three waves of the internationalization of the U.S. field of curriculum. The first wave was the consolidation and crisis of the field in the 1950s and 1960s and its exportation as a new technology-driven curriculum reform in the 1960s; the second was the reconceptualization of the U.S. field by opening itself to mainly European and Latin American international intellectual influences; and finally the third wave is the present moment and the internationalization movement. These waves are not fixed historical stages but tendencies that are still present in the field with different emphases.

During the first wave of internationalization, the field of curriculum arrived in *Latinoamérica*. The concept of curriculum in *Latinoamérica* is inherited from the 1960s when *curriculum development* was imported and adopted from the United States and used to inform educational reforms in the region. That international deployment of this educational discourse meant a mechanistic application of concepts and procedures brought from outside without consideration of local contexts and cultures. Curriculum Studies, therefore, arrived into *Latinoamérica* as a cultural monologue rather than an intercultural dialogue, a sort of suppression of knowledges that Paraskeva (2016, p. 4) has called "curriculum epistemicides." The effects of that story are still to be told. While it is important to recognize that this is not our current understanding of curriculum internationalization, nevertheless this tendency is still strong worldwide. *Latinoamérica* is, then, a worthwhile reminder to the scholars in the field that the first wave of internationalization in Curriculum Studies was a neocolonial one, and that the effort to overcome it is an ongoing one.

That first wave of internationalization began in the 1960s but unevenly reached every Latin American country in the following decades, making this process of importation to have variations from one country to another. While in Chile, for instance, the process started in the context of an educational reform led by a democratic government, in Brazil the field was introduced during the military dictatorship that had taken over in 1964. Nevertheless, the general context was an increasing intervention of the United States in the region under the Cold War rationale. In the intellectual production of Latin American curriculum scholars, this wave of internationalization has been termed "acculturation" (Garcia-Garduño, 2011), an act of "cultural imperialism"[3] (Díaz-Barriga & García-Garduño, 2014, p. 11), the introduction of the "U.S. industrial pedagogy" (Díaz-Barriga, 1984), the beginning of the influence of the "educational technology" expressed for instance in Tyler's work (Magendzo, Abraham, & Lavín, 2014, p. 176), and the technical curriculum (Montoya-Vargas, 2014). Before this wave, "the traits of a view of education based on efficiency and productivity were absent" (p. 11) in *Latinoamérica*, conclude Díaz-Barriga and García-Garduño (2014) in their study of the historical development of Curriculum Studies in ten Latin American countries.

The 1970s reconceptualization of the North Anglo-American curriculum field of Curriculum Studies was a second wave of internationalization. Unlike the first wave, this second wave may be seen as having a different direction, an outside-inside movement rather than the inside-outside dynamic of the previous neocolonial wave. This process of reconceptualization meant for the U.S. curriculum field a paradigmatic shift "from [a] focus on social engineering and the business model to the project of understanding, which involves the concept of curriculum as conversation" (Pinar, 2004, p. 19). The U.S. reconceptualization was a movement nourished by European and British intellectual influences. The reconceptualization sought to understand curriculum "historically, politically, racially, autobiographically or biographically, aesthetically, theologically, institutionally and internationally, as well as in terms of gender, phenomenology, postmodernism, and poststructuralism" (Pinar, 2008, p. 493). All of those schools of thought reflected European traditions brought to the United States in order to help in the project of theorizing curriculum. These were not the only foreign influences in the reconceptualization of Curriculum Studies. In addition to those, Paulo Freire was a strong inspiration from the outset of that process beginning in the 1970s (Greene, 1971; Pinar & Grumet, 1976), a Latin American one (Johnson-Mardones, 2015). Therefore, this second wave of internationalization was not only European but also Latin American. Somehow, put into perspective, these influences advanced the idea of internationalization as a conversation among equals and the hybridity of the field of Curriculum Studies. These beginning strides toward an international conversation, however, faded in the following years. As the United States reconceptualization movement (Pinar & Grumet, 1976; Pinar, Reynolds, Slattery, & Taubman, 1995) and a Latin American pedagogy evolved (Freire, 1970/2000; Dussel, 1980), the initial Freirean dialogical encounter (Freire, 1970/2000; Greene, 1971; Pinar & Grumet, 1976) evaporated as the two countries developed separately and with little interaction. This work is an effort to bring that conversation back together.

As early as the 1960s a similar process of external influences and internal developments that did not subscribe to instrumental or technocratic approaches, but were rather critical of them, took place in *Latinoamérica*. These approaches were both a reaction to the instrumental arrival of the field of curriculum and an effort of thinking about education within our own tradition. In fact, in the following decade those developments were already part of the Latin American educational tradition and affected the reception of the new imported field of curriculum. García-Garduño (2011) terms this second moment in *Latinoamérica* "hybridization." He writes:

> An Argentinean anthropologist living in Mexico, Néstor García Canclini, coined a concept that can help us understand the *mestizaje* or fusion that the curriculum field has undergone since the 1973 Spanish translation of Tyler´s *Basic Principles of Curriculum and Instruction*. García Canclini [2000] understands by hybridity "sociocultural processes where discrete structures or practices that existed separately combine themselves to generate new structures, objects and practices."
>
> (García-Garduño, 2011, p. 16)[4]

This Latin American hybridization of Curriculum Studies, which happened not without contradictions, can be temporally located in the 1970s and 1980s, with various developments depending on each context. The imported curriculum technology of the first wave was little by little "adopting, adapting, syncretizing, rejecting and rearticulating" (Díaz-Barriga & García-Garduño, 2014, p. 12) in the context of the increasing expansion and diversification of the educational system. This hybridity was not only the result of external intellectual influences. As it was already affirmed here, the Latin American critique of modern schooling had commenced in the 1960s by, among others, Paulo Freire and Ivan Illich. It is a quite "paradoxical situation" (Díaz-Barriga & García-Garduño, 2014, p. 12) that this Latin American critique coincided with the first wave of internationalization. Not closed to external influences, this critique had a clear Latin American vocation, given both its perspective and geographical presence. To the works of Illich, written in Mexico, and those of Freire written in Brazil and Chile, we can add others, such as those of the so-called *grupo cordobés*, the Cordoba group, that reflected on "methodological aspects of teaching, apart from technical rationality" (Feeney, 2014, p. 21). Along these lines, Díaz-Barriga and García-Garduño (2014) describe the Mexican context:

> The development of critical perspective in curriculum was a hybrid process led by young scholars, recently arrived from Argentina, such as Azucena Rodríguez, Alfredo Furlán, Eduardo Remedi y Roberto Follari; and young Mexican curriculum scholars such as Ángel Díaz-Barriga, Patricia Aristi y Alicia De Alba.
>
> (pp. 250–251)[5]

All these processes made the field of curriculum hybrid, or better, enabled the field of curriculum in *Latinoamérica* to have its own hybridization, since, in general, the influence of the U.S. hybridization—namely the reconceptualization movement of the 1970s—reached those landscapes at least two decades later. A paradigmatic case in this regard is the scholarship of William F. Pinar, the main figure of the reconceptualization, whose work has not been translated into Spanish until recently, having had then only an indirect influence in the Spanish-speaking world. Only one book, which collects several translated essays, was published on the initiative of the Mexican curriculum scholar García-Garduño in 2014.[6] Therefore, all this "was enabling the conformation of a distinctive curriculum thought, with an element that gives identity: it sought to be Latin American" (Díaz-Barriga & García-Garduño, 2014, p. 252). As incomplete as this introductory paragraph may be, it allows a look at both the hybridity and Latino Americanness of Curriculum Studies in our *Latinoamérica mestiza*.

The current internationalization movement is the third wave, which has interests in the study of Curriculum Studies outside of the United States (Pinar, 2014c) as well as in theorizing the idea of a worldwide non-uniform field (Pinar, 2014c; Miller, 2009). This process has been dominated by national accounts of the situation of Curriculum Studies in different countries. The publication of the two editions of the *Handbook of International Curriculum Research* (Pinar, 2003, 2014c) have been great contributions in this regard. The next step is to develop international or transnational research on curriculum focused on the interrelationships among national developments and their discontinuities. It is within this interpretive space that a more comprehensive theory of curriculum and education can emerge. Nevertheless, this movement still struggles with a propensity to normalize "the linguistic, cultural, and racial differences under the authoritative canon of Euro-American rationality" (Ropo & Autio, 2009, p. 3). Nevertheless, the process is already underway.

It is in this third wave of internationalization that the field of Curriculum Studies seems to be recovering the dialogical encounter that began with the critiques of technocratic curriculum characteristic of the first wave of internationalization, and the reconceptualization movement saw as a way of raising consciousness. García-Garduño (2011) speaks also of a moment of internationalization and cosmopolitanism in Curriculum Studies in Latin America:

> In the case of Ibero-América, there are indications that processes of cosmopolitanism are underway. However, they are not completely clear. The most outstanding traits of cosmopolitanism are openings to other trends and scholarship, the acceptance of different points of view without losing one's own. Curriculum journals that exist in Brazil and in Spain publish articles from both Latin American and Anglo-Saxon scholars.
>
> (García-Garduño, 2011, p. 16)

Although the Latin American intellectual production on the internationalization of Curriculum Studies is still limited, it has increased during the decade of 2010. Important works have been published on Brazil (Pinar, 2011b) and Mexico (Pinar, 2011c). Both texts comprise chapters by the main scholars in the field in each country, providing a broad view of the curriculum discourses in those contexts. *The International Handbook of Curriculum Research* (Pinar, 2003) also includes chapters on Argentina (Feeney & Terigi, 2003; Feldman & Palamidessi, 2003), Brazil (Moreira, 2003; Casimiro & Macedo, 2003), and Mexico (Díaz-Barriga, 2003a). The second edition of this handbook (2014) has expanded its Latin American spectrum, adding chapters on Colombia (Montoya-Vargas, 2014), on Chile (Matus, 2014), and Peru (Manrique, Revilla, & Lamas, 2014). Besides these works published in English, we find works in Portuguese such as that of Moreira on Brazil (2007) and in Spanish such as Díaz-Barriga's (2003b, 2002, 1991, 1982) on Mexico. In addition, two important works have been published recently in *Latinoamérica*: *Desarrollo del Curriculum en América Latina: Experiencia de Diez Países* (2014) [Historical Development of Curriculum in Latin America: The Experience of Ten Countries] by Díaz-Barriga and García-Garduño (Eds.); and *Diálogos Curriculares entre México y Brasil* [Curricular Dialogues between Mexico and Brazil] (2015) by Alicia De Alba and Alice Casimiro Lopes (Eds.).

So far, I have grounded my understanding of internationalization as a dimension of the field of curriculum here by juxtaposing the historical development of the field in the United States in relation to *Latinoamérica* and the historical development of the field there. I would like to suggest again that the next step to building an international field of

Curriculum Studies is enlarging the conversation beyond its Anglo-Saxon and European influences. Therefore, my work must be understood as an attempt to bring the Latin American educational tradition more strongly into the international conversation that is now Curriculum Studies. In doing so, I am, to some extent, rejoining two educational traditions, the Latina American and the Anglo-American, to continue a conversation already begun in the 1970s but interrupted since then. I restore the concept of dialogical encounter as a fundamental practice in times of planetary agony. In the same Freirean fashion, my writing aims to solve no problem but to pose many.

My Search for a Method

In my search for a method to study the lived curriculum, I have studied biographical approaches in Curriculum Studies and Qualitative Inquiry. As a result, I have learned about correspondences between *currere*[7] (Pinar, 1976) and *interpretive autoethnography* (Denzin, 1989, 2013a, 2013b). It is Sartre's *Search for a Method* (1963) that informs both Pinar's and Denzin's searches. Both authors draw on the "regressive-progressive and analytic-synthetic method;" the existentialist method, as Sartre termed it (1963, p. 148). This common source focuses on the understanding of life and history in their intersection. Sartre affirms that existentialism "discovers the point of insertion for man and his class—that is, the particular family—as mediation between the universal class and the individual" (1963, p. 62). According to him, it is the integration of psychoanalysis that enables the deployment of a method with the possibility of understanding social life. Pinar draws on Sartre's *Search for a Method* to understand the inner experience of external structures in education. Drawing also on Sartre, Denzin (1989, 2013a, 2013b) searches for a method that "allows the researcher to take each person's life in its immediate particularity and to ground that life in its historical moment" (Denzin, 2013b, p. 124). Thus, Pinar's *currere* and Denzin's *interpretive autoethnography* seek to understand how life and history intertwine. The individual then emerges as an historical subject both constrained but also able to read and transform the world, to use Freire's words. In consonance with those methodological approaches, Freire also reminds us, that for human beings "as historical, autobiographical, 'beings for themselves,' their transformation occurs in their own existential time, never outside it" (Freire, 1970/2000, p. 16). And because existential time is historical, we and the society we live in can be transformed. On the other hand, in a context where human beings' historicity is denied, women and men are "divided between an identical past and present, and a future without hope" (Freire, 1970/2000, p. 173). But when "men [and women] emerge from time, discover temporality, and free themselves from 'today,' their relations with the world become impregnated with consequence" (Freire,

1973, p. 4). It is in that "existential time" that Freire calls for recovering our human biographical-historical consciousness.

The biographical perspective was also an explicit concern for Freire. Actually, the idea of writing an autobiographical text was part of Freire's considerations from a very early time. He intended to write an autobiography in the late 1960s, when he wrote his first works; a story recalled in the 1980s in his coauthored *Aprendendo Com a Própria História* (Freire & Guimarães, 1987) [Learning from our own history]. It is interesting that in Portuguese, as in Spanish, *História* means both history and story, which emphasizes the non-separable connection that life and history have for Freire. Nevertheless, it was not until the 1990s that the project of an autobiographical text became a reality in his *Letters to Cristina: Reflections on My Life and Work* (1996). This autobiographical writing took the form of letters to his nice Cristina who had asked him to write her letters about his childhood and youth for her to understand how he had become the educator that he was.

The autobiographical is already present in Freire's main writings in first person narratives about personal-professional experiences that show us how his educational theory was developed. This characteristic of Freire's speaking-writing has not gone unnoticed. One of his first biographers in the United States claims that his "thought evolves from his early family life and education and from his reflections upon those experiences and the experiences of those with whom he worked and lived" (Collins, 1977, p. 4). This same autobiographical trait led to another scholar (Taylor, 1993) naming Freire's writing as a "bio-text." He explains why he "preferred to use the term 'bio-text' rather than biography. First, because Freire has always insisted on writing his own life in his own script" (p. 3). As we can see, autobiographical reflection is also part of Freire's methodological and pedagogical approach. The variant of *currere* I am proposing is Freirean in this way.

Currere

Curriculum as lived is lived experience, a concept that Pinar (1976) associates with the German concept of *Lebenswelt*. *Lebenswelt* can be translated as life-world or the world of lived experience. "This *lebenswelt*, the experience of the educational journey; it is the study of curriculum reconceived, that is, *currere*" (Pinar, 1976, p. 18). *Currere* is the Latin root of the word curriculum, which means to run the course; "curriculum reconceptualized in *currere*: it is not the course to be run, or the artifacts we use in the running of the course; it is the running of the course" (Pinar, 1976, p. 18). In addition, *currere* is the experience of studying or having studied the course. The use of the verbal form stresses the dynamic character of *currere* in opposition to the static nature of the noun *curriculum*. By introducing the complexity of life as an educational concern, curriculum is no longer static (prescribed) but dynamic (lived). That is why the use of the verb form of *currere* is to be preferred to the noun *curriculum* in Curriculum Studies. The dialectic between the prescribed and the lived becomes the central focus of the study of curriculum. The concept of "*currere* forefronts the meaning of the curriculum as complicated conversation encouraging educational experience" (Pinar, 2011a, p. 2). It is in the interplay of the planned curriculum and the curriculum as lived that the conversation about one's education becomes complicated; and that complicated conversation is what curriculum is about. *Currere* is the curriculum actually lived by a student. This emphasis on the personal dimension of schooling is different from the discursive presence of the "individual" as an abstract entity, an ideal to be reached. *Currere* refers to the "existential experience of external structures" (Pinar & Grumet, 1976, p. vii). Drawing on that understanding, in this study I am concerned about my and others' "existential experience," personal and social as well as emotional and intellectual, of the "external structures," both disciplinary and socio-historical. Again, my departure point is my own doctoral experience. After all, *currere* "is a reflective cycle in which thought bends back upon itself and thus recovers its volition" (Grumet, 1976a, p. 70) opening a space for understanding.

This conversation is also complicated in intergenerational terms. Our educational experience takes place in the borderland between two realms. We live our life in the liminal space between our predecessor's and successor's realms. Our lived educational experience is lived in the threshold of our successors' and ancestors' realms, to use Schutz's expression. The *lebenswelt* is then an intergenerational space making *curriculum* a matter of an active reception, that is the reinvention, of a given. That is also the situation of an academic field understood as a socio-intellectual community; it is an intergenerational conversation in which there is an attempt to pass on a legacy while reinventing it at the same time. In that sense, *currere* becomes "the site on which the generations struggle to define themselves and the world" (Pinar et al., 1995, p. 849); a liminal space (Sameshima & Irwin, 2008) in which one needs to be fully present and willing to engage in dialogical encounters. To me, as it does for others, that struggle requires the study of the past, my own and the field's, in order to understand the present and imagine a better future. Our inner experience of the external structures becomes a stance from which we talk about the educational context, nationally and globally. In other words, understanding requires the will to listen to the whole conversation in the field; to listen to a "cacophony of voices" (Pinar et al., 1995, p. xiii) from both the center and the periphery, and beyond. As a graduate student, therefore, I was seeking to join a conversation not only already started but also multiple, disconnected, and sometimes even incoherent. People in that conversation keep talking, making it harder for me, and for everyone, to catch up on everything, every time, everywhere.

Thus, a field is not a single, simple conversation but many. Those multiple conversations require us to converse across them, in order to develop our capacity to participate in the field. In that sense, our academic journey takes us through varied lands named differently by a multiplicity of ownership claims. Moreover, our fellow travelers speak also in a variety of languages, making the conversation even more complicated, more difficult to share the notes we keep in our journals, and to read the maps that we and they carry. It is this situation, perhaps, that has also led us to think of the field of curriculum as complicated conversation, and perhaps to think of any field as a conversation.

Therefore, situating myself in the field of Curriculum Studies as an international conversation, I suggest a variant of the method of *currere*. In surveying a life, told orally or written, *currere* sorts images and stories of someone's past, present, and future in order to understand and reconstruct it. First one's past is activated. This is the first moment, the *regressive*. The *regressive* looks backward, revisiting the past that was once inhabited. The second moment is the *progressive*, the time to imagine the future. It is the time to see ourselves there, dwelling in a place that is not yet. In the *analytical*, the third moment, our present is bracketed in order for one to be released from experience. Each of these moments is conceived as a "now time," as a picture that fixes time, allowing it to be seen. Then history appears as "the presence of the now" (Benjamin, 1968, p. 261), epiphanies in someone's life-history span, Denzin would add. This makes it possible to see what is, what was, and what is not yet. Now, life can be read and re-written. The last step is the *synthetic*. This is the time to see oneself as concrete and to put everything together. In Sartre's (1963) words, it is the moment when "superimposed significations isolated and enumerated by analysis require now to be joined together in life" (p. 108). This kind of moment, as I understand it, are exceptional in life.

I deploy my understanding of curriculum as *currere* (Pinar, 1976; Grumet, 1976a) to inform my study conceptually and methodologically. In *currere*, the phenomenon concerning Curriculum Studies has been re-defined as lived educational experience. In addition, *currere* is also a method developed to study that phenomenon. This understanding helps in my attempt to develop an international conversation between the U.S. and Latin American educational traditions. I explore the connections between the historical developments of the field in the United States and in Latin America since the 1960s. I will try to understand my biographical situation as a Latin American history teacher earning a Ph.D. in Curriculum and Instruction in a U.S. university. This undertaking finds insight in that of Pinar and Grumet (1976) at the beginning of the scholarship on *currere*. They write,

> We will attempt to describe educational experience in its most particularized incarnation, the history and response of the individual

[my educational experience], and in its most general expression, the interpretation of human experience that characterizes the conceptual frameworks of the disciplines [Curriculum Studies] that shape educational research.

(Pinar & Grumet, 1976, p. viii)

In my case, my biography intertwines with the field's history. I focus on my own life and the intellectual history of Curriculum Studies as an academic field. The most "particular incarnation" of curriculum as lived experience (myself) is put in relation with the "most general expression" of it (Curriculum Studies), which is the discipline I am coming to profess.

In addition, I must say that in the effort of developing this international conversation in Curriculum Studies, I find inspiration in Pinar's insightful undertaking in the second edition of *What is Curriculum Theory?* (2012). There, he uses the *regressive-progressive-analytical-synthetical* method of *currere* to understand the field of Curriculum Theory, a subfield within Curriculum Studies. Then, biography becomes allegory, he argues; and the biographical situation of the curriculum theorist is also the historical situation of the field. "Disciplines provide metaphors for daily experience" (Pinar, 1976, p. 76). Drawing on that idea, I tie each of the four moments of *currere* to a specific decade in my life and in the history of the field in the United States and Latin America.

These four moments of *currere* have been joined together into two pairs: the regressive-progressive and the analytical-synthetical. This seeks to avoid any lineal temporality that the association of each moment to a specific decade may suggest. This decision seems also consistent with the concept of force field to describe the tensions of one's intellectual life, comprising temporal and spatial dimensions. Therefore, the *regressive* moment, the time of the given, is tied to the 1960s, the time when the arrival of the field of curriculum takes place, and is put into tension with the *progressive*, tied to the 1990s and the emergence of the Other around the commemoration of 1492. The *analytical* is the 2000s, in which I connect my decision to devote myself to the field of education, and is put in tension with the *synthetical*, which refers to the current moment, the 2010s, as a time when I devote myself to the study of Curriculum Studies. From there, I propose my version of a cosmopolitan project in Curriculum Studies—a cosmopolitanism that I can only sing in a Latin American key.

Regarding the field of intellectual influences informing this project, William F. Pinar appears as the main curriculum scholar whose works are used to develop this international conversation in Curriculum Studies. Paulo Freire is the main author within the educational Latin American tradition. Enrique Dussel is another Latin American author addressed in this work, given his contribution to Latin American thinking and specifically his theorization of the *Pedagógica Latinoamericana* within the philosophy of liberation. The work of Walter Benjamin, especially his concepts of dialectical image and elective affinities, are also fundamental to this endeavor. Somehow, each of these four authors become a sort of proxy to approach the tradition of Anglo-Saxon Curriculum Studies, the tradition of *Pedagogía Latinoamericana,* and the Latin American and European Philosophies.

I have also tried to take the metaphor of conversation seriously, informing my writing as such: I have attempted to develop a conversational way of writing. Richardson and St. Pierre's (2005) insight about writing as inquiry provide a fruitful understanding, since as conversation the writing then must to be practiced to come into being. The use of quotations to perform multivocity has been inspired by Pinar's style and by Denzin's performance texts. The fragmentary fluidity of conversation found inspiration also in Benjamin's understanding of quotations and the metaphor of the collector. I must mention that both Pinar and Denzin draw on Benjamin's concept of montage in their thinking and writing. Finally, Freire's concept of dialogue and particularly his *livros conversa* [conversation books] underlines my intention of blurring the written and spoken world. Therefore, the quotations come from written, mostly, and spoken sources. The spoken materials, mostly stored in my inner conversation, have been translated into written language. They are memories of my past which comprise not only my words but the words of others that have stayed with me.

This text, then, is somehow a montage (Denzin, 1997; Pinar, 2015b) of many and varied texts that have been uttered during my years as a doctoral student. The concern with the concept of field and literature review that is supposed to be a part of a dissertation came first to me during the introductory seminar of the *Unit of Curriculum, Aesthetic, and Teacher Education* that I took along with my cohort during my first year at UIUC. The seminar was led by Dr. Marjory Osborne and most of the professors of CATE and C&I visited the seminar, engaging with us in a conversation whose content was their intellectual biography. The concern would come again at the time of my general exams, when I was taking Dr. Bresler's seminar on *Research in Progress.* Encouraged by her, in that class I presented for the very first time the idea of a dissertation based on a variant of the method of *currere,* that now has been developed into a book. At that point, I had advanced in my study of biographical approaches in Curriculum Studies and Qualitative Inquiry that I began my first year in Marilyn's (Dr. Marilyn Johnston-Parsons, my adviser) class on Narrative Inquiry and Life History. In that class I also had my first encounter with postcolonial theory, of which I had some notice before through the Latin American scholarship on decolonization. That beginning would be later deepened in courses with Dr. Cameron McCarthy on Cultural Studies and Critical Interpretations and on Postcolonial

Theory and Methodology. My study of biographical approaches in Qualitative Inquiry began in Dr. Norman Denzin's seminar on Advanced Interpretive Methods and continued in several subsequent independent studies courses with him on *interpretive autoethnography*. My study of the biographical in Curriculum Studies, and specifically of *currere*, had begun in Chile, continued at Louisiana State University when I started to read books I had only known in reference lists, and became central in Urbana-Champaign in Sue Noffke's (Dr. Susan Noffke) class on *Curriculum Theory and History*. In the previous semester, she had encouraged me to write about Action Research as a form of self-narrative. Another topic in our conversations had been internationalization. That topic had been called upon by Kliebard during Sue's doctoral studies at Wisconsin-Madison. Kliebard wanted to her to write her dissertation on the influences between the German tradition and the U.S. Curriculum Studies, particularly focused on the Herbartians. She did not do that but the historical, theoretical, and international influence of Kliebard remained with her. My study of *currere* was taken to a different level with my encounter with Dr. William F. Pinar, first in his texts that became linguistically and materially available to me on crossing the border; then in the e-mails we started to exchange at the end of my first doctoral year; and then in person during the AERA annual meeting in San Francisco in 2013, when I shared with him my idea of writing a dissertation on the internationalization of Curriculum Studies. Our conversation has continued since then in many conferences in the United States, Canada, China, and Portugal, alongside the international conversation that was taking place in those meetings. Frequent visits to UBC during the years of 2014–2016 have helped to keep our conversation going and to enrich my study.

This Book

My work addresses the field of Curriculum Studies as a worldwide interdisciplinary field, its difficulties, complications, and possibilities. It primarily focuses on the relations between the Anglo-Saxon field of Curriculum Studies and the Latin American educational tradition. Looking at these relations from the 1960s to the current moment, I seek to unpack the complexities involved in understanding Curriculum Studies as an international academic field. Although there are historical and current power dynamics complicating this endeavor, I suggest a possible cosmopolitan project informed by intercultural dialogue to develop inter-transnational scholarship on Curriculum Studies.

Methodologically, I suggest a variant of the *regressive-progressive-analytical-synthetical* method *currere*. I tie each of these four moments of *currere* to a specific decade in my life and in the history of the field in the United States and Latin America. The *regressive* moment, the time of the given, is tied to the 1960s, when the field of curriculum arrived and was in tension with the *progressive* moment, which is tied to the 1990s and the problem of "the other" that emerged around the commemoration of 1492. The *analytical* is the 2000s, in which the decision to devote myself to the field of education was put into tension with the *synthetical*, which refers to the current moment, the 2010s, when I advocate the study of Curriculum Studies. From there, I propose my version of a cosmopolitan project in Curriculum Studies.

In this first chapter, I have offered an introduction to the project of understanding Curriculum Studies as an international conversation. I have sketched the main insights informing my proposal in theoretical and methodological terms. I focused first on the meaning of professing an academic field. Then, I addressed the idea of curriculum as *currere* and the meaning of the internationalization of the field of curriculum. I have also explained some choices I made regarding the way to address my study whose written form I present here. Chapter 2 performs a theoretical *détente*. *Détente*, a French word meaning release from tension, helps me to address the main words I use to name my project of bringing together different traditions. As I explain, these words become the gravitational center of my force field of theoretical influences. This chapter also speaks of the intellectual activity that a moment of repose enables before jumping into writing as inquiry. Chapter 3 focuses on the *regressive-progressive*. I begin with my current biographical-historical situation. I describe the present as *given* and the process of becoming historical begins. The present as *given* is also the time when a new generation in Chile started its struggle for a better education for all—a present where curriculum struggled to remain in conversation. Situating in such a "presentistic" present, a context that denies its historicity, marked by a paralyzing attitude, I look backward to the 1960s as a regressive time in history where the technological conception of education was overwhelmingly deployed through the arrival of the curriculum field into Latin America. I look backward to the prehistory of my life, the historical given in which I came into life. In that also "presentistic" present, the regressive 1960s, I found the first talking back to that instrumental educational rationality in both Latin America and shortly after in the United States. My first encounter with the content of schooling occurred within a dictatorship sponsored by the same entity that sponsored the arrival of the field of curriculum in the region. In that regressive time, the memory of students protests everywhere resonate in scholars and laypeople. In today's regressive time more recent student protests, particularly in 2011 in Chile, resonate with that past, with my past, my present, screaming [a] future. The *regressive* reading of the 1960s is put into tension by the *progressive* conceptualization of the 1990s, a time when *Latinoamérica* witnessed the emergence of the *Otro* as a legitimate other. Rejecting the celebration of 500 years of discovery of America in 1992, many called to celebrate their 500 years of resistance. I lived that historical moment in relation with history and theology as academic disciplines, more precisely with my study of Latin American history and liberation theology. Through that path I came into the field of education. Chapter 4 is the *analytical-synthetical* pair of *currere*. Turning the century, I was fully in the field of education. Participating as a teacher educator in teacher training programs moved me into a dialogue between the Didactic of History and Social Sciences[8] and Curriculum Studies, particularly Curriculum Theory. Those programs were part of the implementation of the 1990s' Chilean curriculum reform. The curriculum reform had reached all levels of schooling and was moving to higher education and particularly to teacher education. Standardization and accountability were the unmistakable emphasis of a reform in which democracy seemed to be briefly taught rather than profoundly lived. This was the time in which the movement of internationalization of Curriculum Studies started, a movement whose name opposed globalization as recolonization and its neo-imperialistic fashion. The *analytic* moment of taking apart is followed by one of reconstruction. I connect that moment to my coming to profess a field which I understand as an international conversation. Through the study of this interdisciplinary international field, I write my way out of that history of negation of *Latinoamérica* as *Otro*. Talking from that hybrid southerner space, I engage in the developing of an international conversation that shapes a cosmopolitan project in Curriculum Studies. It is a project that needs to move the field to study and learn from and with other western and non-western traditions such as German *Didaktik* and Chinese wisdom. Finally, Chapter 5 is the conclusion. I think of the conclusion as an afterword reflection upon what I have written, the final stage of writing as inquiry, the beginning of the afterlife of the text. Hence I begin with a reflection on my writing. Then, I address three concepts that emerge from that work: hybridity, cosmopolitism, and translation. I suggest that a cosmopolitan project in Curriculum Studies can be reached in the liminal space of translation, and particularly in the translation of those untranslatables that exist in every culture. Those are the words that trigger conversation and keep it going. I also suggest possible developments of this initial work.

A Remark

In my personal journey, I have come to understand curriculum as a field focused on the study of educational experience. I have accepted, not unproblematically, Pinar's conceptualization of the field of Curriculum Studies as a complicated conversation about our educational experience; that is, curriculum as *currere*. I have also situated my joining that conversation from an international point of view, from my Latin-American self. It is my own biography that brings this particular conversation into being. The departure point is my existential situation and the desire to make sense of it, the intention of making life educative by looking backward to figure out a new space for understanding. Therefore, I situate my own educational experience at the center of this inquiry. I try to understand my biographical situation as a Latin American history teacher earning a Ph.D. in Curriculum and Instruction in an American university, a context where my biography intertwines with the field's history. I move from biography to history in a complicated conversation where personal troubles become public issues, biography and history intertwine, and the struggle for a better life emerges with ethical urgency.

Notes

1. As I have explained in another work, I use the expression "Latin American thinker of liberation" "to refer to the intellectual work of a generation whose main concern was to think Latin American from its specificity. This was the project that now is known as the "decolonizing turn" (Castro-Gómez & Grosfoguel, 2007; Dussel, 2013, 2011; Mignolo, 2011), "a new epistemological 'location' for our themes" (Dussel, 2011, p. 188). Liberation was the concept used by these Latin American intellectuals to think several disciplines through Latin American lenses back in the 1960s and 1970s. Fals Borda wrote his *Liberation Sociology* (1968) in Colombia, Gustavo Gutiérrez published his *Theology of Liberation* (1970) in Peru, Enrique Dussel wrote his *Philosophy of Liberation* (1980) already in exile in Mexico. Paulo Freire wrote also within this tradition, stating in his *Pedagogy of the Oppressed* (1970) that "the central problem is this: How can the oppressed, as divided, unauthentic beings, participate in developing the pedagogy of their liberation?" (p. 48) (Johnson-Mardones, 2016, p. 3).
2. The first historical moment (Pinar, 2008) is the age of curriculum as *curriculum development*. This moment is characterized for the dominance that what is now known as Tyler's rationale. This moment begins with the Bobbitt's *The Curriculum* (1918), is consolidated by Tyler's *The Basic Principles of Curriculum and Instruction* (1949), and then fell into crisis since the 1960s. Perhaps, the commonplace of locating the birth of the field with Bobbitt is a clear indicator of the technocratic "essence" that characterizes curriculum as curriculum development. But, why is it Bobbitt and not Dewey referred to as the father of field? Some could ask. Actually Dewey's *The Child and the Curriculum* (1902) was published 16 years before *The Curriculum* (1918), and we are talking about the main educational thinker in the United States; a point made but not developed by Jackson (1992) in his historical review of the field. Following up in this idea, we may say that Tyler's "Principles" (1949) signals the consolidation of the field as an educational technology given his move of tying educational objectives to evaluation.
3. Díaz-Barriga and García-Garduño (2014) refer the term "cultural imperialism" to the work of Martin Carnoy (1993) *La educación como imperialismo cultural* [Educatión as cultural imperialism].
4. Free translation.
5. Free Translation.
6. Pinar's essay (1978) on the reconceptualization of the field was included in an edited book by Gimeno Sacristán y Pérez Gómez (1985) which also included other important works by curriculum scholars.
7. My first encounter with word *currere* occurred during my Master's program in Curriculum Studies at the University of Chile. I was looking for a way to

connect Curriculum Theory and teacher education research. I had read a quote in an article that had captivated me: "There is no better way to study curriculum than to study ourselves" (Connelly and Clandinin, quoted in Pinar, 2008, p. 498) that helped me to think of curriculum as what is lived rather than what is prescribed. Life history appeared to be a good methodology to look at that phenomenon. However, it continued to be problematic how to develop a concept of lived curriculum that allowed me to link teacher education and Curriculum Theory. Then I found a paper by William F. Pinar entitled *The Method of Currere*, presented at the 1975 AERA annual meeting. There, curriculum was understood as *currere*, as a complicated conversation about one's educational experience, while being also a method to study that experience. I had found a concept that enabled me to connect Curriculum Theory and teacher education. It also awakened my interest to investigate the field of curriculum more deeply, to understand what curriculum as "complicated conversation" meant; and it also expanded my interests in biographical and narrative approaches in qualitative inquiry.
8. This field, and especially the class in teacher education programs, is the equivalent in the Spanish-speaking world to the class on teaching, methods in specific fields in teacher education programs in the United States.

References

Aoki, T. (2005). *Curriculum in a new key: The collected works of Ted T. Aoki*. Mahwah, NJ: Lawrence Erlbaum Associates.
Apple, M. W. (1979). *Ideology and curriculum*. London: Routledge & Kegan Paul.
Autio, T. (2006). *Subjectivity, curriculum and society: Between and beyond German Didaktik and Anglo-American curriculum studies*. Mahwah, NJ: Lawrence Erlbaum Associates.
Benjamin, W. (1968). *Illuminations*. New York, NY: Schocken Books.
Bobbitt, F. (1918). *The curriculum*. Boston: Houghton Mifflin.
Carnoy, M. (1993). *La educación como imperialismo cultural*. México: Siglo XXI.
Casimiro Lopes, A., & Macedo, E. (2003). The curriculum field in Brazil since the 1990s. In W. F. Pinar (Ed.). *International handbook of curriculum research* (1st ed., pp. 86–100). Mahwah, NJ: Lawrence Erlbaum Associates.
Castro-Gómez, S., & Grosfoguel, R. (Eds.) (2007). *El giro decolonial: Reflexiones para una diversidad epistémica más allá del capitalismo global*. Bogotá, DC: Siglo del Hombre.
Collins, D. E. (1977). *Paulo Freire, his life, works, and thought*. New York, NY: Paulist Press.
Connelly, F. M., He, M. F., & Phillion, J. (Eds.) (2008). *The Sage handbook of curriculum and instruction*. Los Angeles, CA: Sage Publications.
De Alba, A., & Casimiro Lopes, A. (Eds.) (2015). *Diálogos curriculares entre México y Brasil*. México: Universidad Nacional Autónoma de México.
Denzin, N. K. (2013a). Interpretive autoethnography. In S. L. Holman Jones & C. Ellis (Eds.). *Handbook of autoethnography* (pp. 123–142). New York, NY: Left Coast Press.
Denzin, N. K. (2013b). *Interpretive autoethnography*. Thousand Oaks, CA: Sage Publications.
Denzin, N. K. (1997). Performance texts. In W. G. Tierney & Y. S. Lincoln (Eds.). *Representation and the text: Re-framing the narrative voice*. Albany, NY: State University of New York Press.

Denzin, N. K. (1989). *Interpretive biography*. Newbury Park, CA: Sage Publications.
Denzin, N. K., & Lincoln, Y. S. (Eds.) (2011). *The Sage handbook of qualitative research*. Thousand Oaks, CA: Sage Publications.
De Sousa Santos, B. (2014). *Epistemologies of the South: Justice against epistemicide*. London: Routledge.
Dewey, J. (1902). *The child and the curriculum*. Chicago, IL: University of Chicago Press.
Díaz-Barriga, A. (2003a). Curriculum research: Evolution and outlook in Mexico. In Pinar (Ed.). *Handbook of research on curriculum* (1st ed., pp. 443–446). Mahwah, NJ: Lawrence Erlbaum Associates.
Díaz-Barriga, A. (2003b). *La investigación curricular en México: La década de los noventa* (pp. 63–123). En Consejo Mexicano de Investigación Educativa (Ed.). *La investigación educativa en México*. México: Consejo Mexicano de Investigación Educativa.
Díaz-Barriga, A. (2002). Curriculum: Una mirada sobre sus desarrollos y retos. In I. Westbury (Ed.). *Hacia dónde va el curriculum? La contribución de la teoría deliberadora* (pp. 163–175). Barcelona: Ediciones Pomares.
Díaz-Barriga, A. (1991). Desarrollo del discurso curricular en México. En A. de Alba, A. Díaz-Barriga, & E. González Gaudiano. *El campo del curriculum: Antología* (pp. 7–11). México: CESU-UNAM.
Díaz-Barriga, A. (1984). *Didáctica y Curriculum*. México: Ediciones Nuevo Mar.
Díaz-Barriga, A. (1982). La evolución del discurso curricular en México (1970–1982): El caso de la educación superior. *Revista Latinoamericana de Estudios Educativos, 15*(2), 67–79.
Díaz-Barriga, A., & García-Garduño, J. M. (2014). *Desarrollo del curriculum en América Latina: Experiencia de diez países*. Buenos Aires: Miño y Dávila editores.
Dussel, E. (2013). *Ethics of liberation in the age of globalization and exclusion*. Durham: Duke University Press.
Dussel, E. (2011). *Politics of liberation: A critical world history*. London: SCM Press.
Dussel, E. (1985). *Philosophy of liberation*. New York, NY: Orbis Books.
Dussel, E. (1980). *La pedagógica latinoamericana*. Bogotá: Editorial Nueva América.
Dussel, E. (1976). *History and the theology of liberation: A Latin America perspective*. Maryknoll, NY: Orbis Books.
Dussel, E. (1973). *Para una ética de la liberación latinoamericana*. Buenos Aires: Siglo Veintiuno Argentina Editores. V1.
Fals Borda, O. (1968). *Sociología de la liberación*. Bogotá: Siglo XXI.
Fanon, F. (2004). *The wretched of the earth*. New York, NY: Grove Press.
Feeney, S. (2014). Los estudios del curriculum en Argentina: Particularidades de una disputa académica. In A. Díaz-Barriga & J. M. García-Garduño (2014). *Desarrollo del curriculum en América Latina: Experiencia de diez países* (pp. 15–44). Buenos Aires: Miño y Dávila editores.
Feeney, S., & Terigi, F. (2003). Curriculum studies in Argentina: Documenting the constitution of a field. In W. F. Pinar (Ed.). *Handbook of research on curriculum* (1st ed., pp. 101–108). Mahwah, NJ: Lawrence Erlbaum Associates.
Feldman, D., & Palamidessi, M. (2003). The development of curriculum thought in Argentina. In W. F. Pinar (Ed.). *Handbook of research on curriculum* (1st ed., pp. 109–122). Mahwah, NJ: Lawrence Erlbaum Associates.

Freire, P. (1996). *Letters to Cristina: Reflections on my life and work*. New York, NY: Routledge.
Freire, P. (1973). *Education for critical consciousness*. New York, NY: Seabury Press.
Freire, P. (1970/2000). *Pedagogy of the oppressed*. New York, NY: Continuum.
Freire, P., & Guimarães, S. (1987). *Aprendendo com a própria história*. Rio de Janeiro: Editora Paz e Terra.
García Canclini, N. (2000). *Hybrid cultures: Strategies for entering and leaving modernity*. Minneapolis, MN: University of Minnesota Press.
García-Garduño, J. M. (2011). The institutionalization of curriculum studies in Mexico: Understanding acculturation, hybridity, cosmopolitanism in Ibero-American curriculum studies. In W. F. Pinar (Ed.). *Curriculum studies in Mexico: Intellectual histories, present circumstances* (pp. 137–164). New York, NY: Palgrave Macmillan.
Gimeno Sacristán, J., & Pérez Gómez, A. (1985). *La enseñanza: Su teoría y su práctica*. Madrid: Akal.
Greene, M. (1971). Curriculum and consciousness. In W. F. Pinar (Ed.) (1975/2000). *Curriculum theorizing: The reconceptualization* (pp. 299–320). Troy, NY: Educator's International Press.
Grumet, M. (1976a). Toward a poor curriculum. In W. F. Pinar & M. R. Grumet. *Toward a poor curriculum* (pp. 67–88). Dubuque, IA: Kendall/Hunt.
Gutierrez, G. (1970). *Teología de la liberación: Perspectivas*. Lima: CEP.
Jackson, P. W. (Ed.) (1992). *Handbook of research on curriculum: A project of the American Educational Research Association*. New York, NY: Macmillan.
Johnson-Mardones, D. (2016). *Critical resonances: The Latin American thinkers of liberation and the Frankfurt School*. Paper presented at the 63rd annual conference of the Southeastern Council of Latin American Studies, SECOLAS, March 9–13, Cartagena de Indias, Colombia.
Johnson-Mardones, D. (2015). Freire and the U.S. reconceptualization: Remembering curriculum as international conversation. *Transnational Curriculum Inquiry*, 12(1), 3–12.
Magendzo, A., Abraham, M., & Lavín, S. (2014). El campo curricular y su expresión en las reformas curriculares en Chile. In A. Díaz-Barriga & J. M. García-Garduño (2014). *Desarrollo del curriculum en América Latina: Experiencia de diez países* (pp. 173–210). Buenos Aires: Miño y Dávila editores.
Malewski, E. L. (Ed.) (2010). *Curriculum studies handbook: The next moment*. New York, NY: Routledge.
Manrique, L., Revilla, D., & Lamas, P. (2014). Theoretical approaches underlying primary education curricula in Peru. In W. F. Pinar (Ed.). *Handbook of research on curriculum* (2nd ed., pp. 376–390). Mahwah, NJ: Lawrence Erlbaum Associates.
Matus, C. (2014). Curricular landscapes, neoliberal densities: Curriculum reform and research in Chile. In W. F. Pinar (Ed.). *Handbook of research on curriculum* (2nd ed., pp. 376–390). Mahwah, NJ: Lawrence Erlbaum Associates.
Mignolo, W. (2011). *The darker side of Western modernity: Global futures, decolonial options*. Durham, NC: Duke University Press.
Miller, J. (2009). Curriculum studies and transnational flows and mobilities: Feminist autobiographical perspectives. In E. Ropo & T. Autio (Eds.). *International conversations on curriculum studies: Subject, society and curriculum* (pp. 43–70). Rotterdam: Sense Publishers.

Montoya-Vargas, J. (2014). Curriculum studies in Colombia. In W. F. Pinar (Ed.). *International handbook of curriculum research* (2nd ed., pp. 134–150). Mahwah, NJ: Lawrence Erlbaum Associates.

Moreira, A. (2007). *Currículos e programas no Brasil*. Sao Paulo: Papirus.

Moreira, A. (2003). The curriculum field in Brazil: Emergence and consolidation. In W. F. Pinar (Ed.). *Handbook of research on curriculum* (1st ed., pp. 171–182). Mahwah, NJ: Lawrence Erlbaum Associates.

Paraskeva, J. M. (2016). *Curriculum epistemicides: Towards an itinerant curriculum theory*. New York, NY: Routledge.

Pinar, W. F. (Ed.) (2015a). *Curriculum studies in India: Intellectual histories, present circumstances*. New York, NY: Palgrave Macmillan.

Pinar, W. F. (2015b). *Educational experience as lived: Knowledge, history, alterity*. New York, NY: Palgrave Macmillan.

Pinar, W. F. (2014a). Curriculum research in the United States: Crisis, reconceptualization, internationalization. In W. F. Pinar (Ed.). *International handbook of curriculum research* (2nd ed., pp. 521–532). Mahwah, NJ: Lawrence Erlbaum Associates.

Pinar, W. F. (Ed.) (2014b). *Curriculum studies in China: Intellectual histories, present circumstances*. New York, NY: Palgrave Macmillan.

Pinar, W. F. (Ed.) (2014c). *International handbook of curriculum research*. Mahwah, NJ: Lawrence Erlbaum Associates.

Pinar, W. F. (2012). *What is curriculum theory?* New York, NY: Routledge.

Pinar, W. F. (2011a). *The character of curriculum studies: Bildung, currere, and the recurring question of the subject*. New York, NY: Palgrave Macmillan.

Pinar, W. F. (Ed.) (2011b). *Curriculum studies in Brazil: Intellectual histories, present circumstances*. New York, NY: Palgrave Macmillan.

Pinar, W. F. (Ed.) (2011c). *Curriculum studies in Mexico: Intellectual histories, present circumstances*. New York, NY: Palgrave Macmillan.

Pinar, W. F. (Ed.) (2010). *Curriculum studies in South Africa: Intellectual histories & present circumstances*. New York, NY: Palgrave Macmillan.

Pinar, W. F. (2008). Curriculum theory since 1950: Crisis, reconceptualization, internationalization. In M. Connelly, M. F. He, & J. Phillion (Eds.). *The Sage handbook of curriculum and instruction* (pp. 491–513). Los Angeles, CA: Sage Publications.

Pinar, W. F. (2006). *The synoptic text today and other essays: Curriculum development after the reconceptualization*. New York, NY: Peter Lang.

Pinar, W. F. (2004). *What is curriculum theory?* Mahwah, NJ: Lawrence Erlbaum Associates.

Pinar, W. F. (Ed.) (2003). *International handbook of curriculum research*. Mahwah, NJ: Erlbaum.

Pinar, W. F. (1978). Notes on the curriculum field. In W. F. Pinar (1994). *Autobiography, politics, and sexuality: Essays in curriculum theory 1972–1992* (pp. 77–100). New York, NY: Peter Lang.

Pinar, W. F. (1976). Self and others. In W. F. Pinar & M. R. Grumet. *Toward a poor curriculum* (pp. 7–30). Dubuque, IA: Kendall/Hunt.

Pinar, W. F., & Grumet, M. (1976). *Toward a poor curriculum*. Dubuque, IA: Kendall/Hunt.

Pinar, W. F., Reynolds, W. M., Slattery, P., & Taubman, P. M. (Eds.) (1995). *Understanding curriculum: An introduction to the study of historical and contemporary curriculum discourses*. New York, NY: Peter Lang.

Popkewitz, T. (Eds.) (2013). *Rethinking the history of education: Transnational perspectives on its questions, methods, and knowledge.* New York, NY: Palgrave Macmillan.

Richardson, L. & St. Pierre, E. A. (2005). Writing: A method of inquiry. In N. K. Denzin & Yvonna S. Lincoln (Eds.). *The SAGE handbook of qualitative research* (pp. 959–978). Thousand Oaks, CA: SAGE Publications.

Ropo, E., & Autio, T. (Eds.) (2009). *International conversations on curriculum studies: Subject, society and curriculum.* Rotterdam: Sense Publishers.

Sameshima, P., & Irwin, R. L. (2008). Rendering dimensions of liminal currere. *Transnational Curriculum Inquiry, 5*(2), 1–15.

Sartre, J. P. (1963). *Search for a method.* New York, NY: Knopf.

Taylor, P. V. (1993). *The texts of Paulo Freire.* Buckingham: Open University Press.

Tröhler, D. (2011). *Languages of education: Protestant legacies, national identities, and global aspirations.* New York, NY: Routledge.

Trueit, D. (Ed.) (2003). *The internationalization of curriculum studies: Selected proceedings from the LSU conference 2000.* New York, NY: Peter Lang.

Tyler, R. W. (1949). *Basic principles of curriculum and instruction.* Chicago, IL: University of Chicago Press.

Wallerstein, I. M. (2004). *World-systems analysis: An introduction.* Durham, NC: Duke University Press.

Weis, L., McCarthy, C., & Dimitriadis, G. (Eds.) (2006). *Ideology, curriculum, and the new sociology of education: Revisiting the work of Michael Apple.* New York, NY: Routledge.

Westbury, I., Hopmann, S., & Riquarts, K. (Eds.) (2000). *Teaching as a reflective practice: The German Didaktik tradition.* Mahwah, NJ: Erlbaum.

Williams, R. (1961). *The long revolution.* London: Columbia University Press.

Yates, L., & Grumet, M. (2011). *World yearbook of education 2011: Curriculum in today's world: Configuring knowledge, identities, work and politics.* New York, NY: Routledge.

2 A Theoretical *Détente*[1]

This chapter aims to perform a theoretical *détente*. *Détente* is a French word meaning release from tension. It is usually used in English to refer to the release of tension in international relationships. Thus, it helps to point to the attitude necessary to forge my understanding of Curriculum Studies as a worldwide educational field. Both the idea of a worldwide field and the attempt to describe it entail listening to different traditions. Bearing the meaning of a repose, rest, and relaxation, the word *détente* conveys that attitude that allows the release of tensions already at play in the relations among those traditions. Those tensions are sorely present within my intellectual force field. My focus is on their resonances rather than their disruptions, although the latter are not ignored. This choice makes it possible for me to achieve the release of tensions and perform this theoretical *détente*.

The word *détente* also speaks to us of the intellectual activity that a moment of repose enables. It resembles the Greek *schole*, as well as the Latin *otium*, and its English equivalent *leisure*. The idea of *scholar*ship seems to be connected to the possibility of having a life that allows *schole*. A distance from the world which enables contemplation of it. Academic activity asks for a life that according to Aristotle seems "to possess self-sufficiency (*autarkos*), time for leisure (*scholastikon*)" (quoted in Dussel, 2011, p. 56). In this sense, Enrique Dussel (2011) has pointed out that scholastikon "signifies those who have rest, peace, serenity, proper to those who withdraw from the city, like the sages in Memphis in Egypt who Aristotle says were the first who had life with schole" (p. 56). This *vita contemplativa* is a good life, a happy life. As a result of this *détente*, scholarship becomes possible. I think of this *détente* as a moment of *vita contemplativa*, a moment and place implied also by the word *theory*. In fact, the word *theory* too speaks of this moment of stillness that makes space for contemplation. As Habermas (1971) reminded us some decades ago, the word *theory* has a religious origin. *Theory* is related to *theoros*, a Greek character commissioned by the *polis* to study other peoples' religious rituals. In order to perform his task, the *theoros* must bracket himself, to allow estrangement. Habermas (1971) writes: "through *theoria*, that is through looking on, he abandons himself to the sacred events. In philosophical language, *theoria* was transferred to contemplation of the cosmos" (p. 301). The *theoros*, Habermas continues, "forms himself through mimesis. Through the soul's likening itself to the ordered motion of the cosmos, theory enters the conduct of life" (pp. 301–302). *Vita contemplativa* is *bio theoretikos*. In my writing, this work of a theoretical *détente* seeks for a moment of *vita contemplativa* at a time in my life when I come to profess an academic discipline that I can only understand as a worldwide field, a sort of life I am aware may not be possible anymore.[2]

Since any academic discipline can be defined as a particular language through which the world is named, to take on a theoretical *détente* when studying an academic discipline entails dealing with language, the words that name the world. The cultivation of that language is the cultivation of the field within the landscapes of experience. That cultivation enables understanding, including self-understanding. Through it, we become what we profess.

It is intriguing that one of the usages of the word *field* in academia refers to the agricultural metaphor. *Field* in this agricultural sense is a landscape made cultural by human intervention seeking the betterment of life. An academic *field* is then a productive unit in the landscapes of culture. The idea of cultivation is at the center of our understanding of knowledge. Alongside the idea of cultivation, however, *field* conveys also the meaning of limits, borders, and divisions. That meaning is also present, though questioned, in our tendency to clearly distinguish between areas of knowledge. As with any other metaphor, therefore, the usage of *field* to conceptualize an academic discipline both opens and closes spaces of meaning. It emphasizes the predominance of the spatial when thinking about our domains of knowledge. It turns us toward the geopolitical. In addition, the agricultural metaphor connects us with the idea of producing knowledge, resting on a certain terrain where cultivation of some sort is possible or suitable, a place we have to go to daily in order to cultivate it. That habit of working daily in the field also changes us. The agricultural metaphor helps us to understand our personal involvement with academic disciplines as a form of cultivation while at the same time it speaks of the disciplinary constraints of such undertaking.

> What would it mean for us to cultivate ourselves "personally," that is, as human subjects, sometimes silenced by distractions of daily lives intensified by the institutions apparently incapable of providing conditions supportive of the calm of contemplation "cultivation" requires.
> (Pinar, 2015, p. 233)

The agricultural meaning of the word *field* is not the only one associated with it, though. The word *field* is also used in physics. This is to think of a *field* as in the idea of a magnetic field or a force field. In this sense, a *field* is a space under the influence of forces that hold its elements together. The idea of a force field is quite appealing to image the intellectual influences informing our academic projects. The U.S. intellectual historian Martin Jay (1984), for instance, has used the metaphor of force field to study the intellectual forces informing Theodor W. Adorno's work. Jay borrows this metaphor from Adorno himself, for whom a force field refers to "a relational interplay of attractions and aversions that constituted the dynamic, transmutational structure of a complex phenomenon" (Jay, 1984, p. 14) such as someone's scholarship. I believe the same usage of the word can be applied to my idea of bringing together the various forces that inform my own intellectual project as expressed in these pages—to invite into the same room authors that are from different "families of the mind" (Sartre, 1963, p. xxxiii). The idea of a force field can characterize more dynamically and flexibly our intellectual influences, superseding the limitation prompted by the use of other conceptualizations such as Lakato's research program (Lakatos, 1978), Kuhn's paradigm (Kuhn, 1962), or even Lauden's traditions (Laudan, 1977). One's intellectual force field is larger than a research program, more permeable than a paradigm, and is likely to cut across several traditions.

The same can be said about the second metaphor used by Jay in his Adorno book: the idea of constellation. According to Jay, this term, which Adorno borrowed from Benjamin, signifies "a juxtaposed rather than integrated cluster of changing elements that resist reduction to a common denominator, essential core, or generative first principle" (Jay, 1984, p. 15). The influences underlying a constellation remain identifiable individually but its legibility comes from their relation to the whole. In his *Force Fields* (1993), Jay argues that the academic discipline he practices "can itself be fruitfully understood as a force field of different impulses" (p. 2). Jay's claim becomes even more suggestive when we think about an academic discipline such as Curriculum Studies as an interdisciplinary and worldwide field—a non-uniform one, Miller (2009) would add. Just as constellations remain unknown before being pointed out and named, academic fields must be shown through the utterance of relations among the forces keeping them together. In fact, thinking of Curriculum Studies as a worldwide field is a case, I believe, in which the metaphor of a force field becomes especially useful, since its situation at the beginning of the twenty-first century has been correctly described as that of a divergent field moving in different directions (Pinar, 2011). The path that I am walking here is leading me to consider that what holds a constellation together is a word or a set of words. In the case of Curriculum Studies the main word seems to be the word naming the field: Curriculum.

My search is *dialogical*. I search *through words*; my search is not yet fully conceptual. Words act to hold force fields together or make them visible. Around those words intellectual traditions gravitate, becoming a force field, a constellation of intellectual influences. At this quantum level of language, words become the gravitational centers of intellectual traditions. Every word acts as a gravitational center around which meanings are held together by a dynamic tension among forces. From a distance, those words seem like stars, but they become constellations when we observe them closely. Accordingly, I will deal with the words I use to name the nature of my study, words I am attaching to myself. Those words make visible my understanding of curriculum as an international conversation: a *conversation* that I enter with my *latinoamericano* body using a variant of the *regressive-progressive-analytical-synthetical* method of *currere*.

Conversation

Etymology tells us that the word conversation means human encounter. It is constructed by the joining of the Latin words *com*—with and *vertere*—to turn. Its direct Latin root is the verb *conversari* which means to live with, to dwell in a place, to turn around. Hence, conversation literally means to turn together, to face each other; and it also means to change together. The biblical use of the word conversation also refers to a collective manner of life, a way of dwelling together. In addition, while in Old English conversation was synonymous with sexual intercourse, today it refers to human intercourse or interaction in general. The word conversation reminds us of the pleasure of human encounters.

Conversation is a human activity. Even better: conversation make us human. Human life is life in conversation. The Chilean biologist Humberto Maturana affirms that conversation is actually the beginning of our humanness. Everything human takes place in conversation. In his *The Origin of Humanness in the Biology of Love* (2008), Maturana explains that language began more than three millennia ago. In those primordial times, he asserts, life in conversation started as a "manner of living" passed on from generation to generation in the small groups in which our ancestors lived. "In fact, [he continues], what must have begun then, must have been living in the braiding of languaging and emotioning that we call conversations" (p. 42). Maturana affirms that in that way human living started as a life lived in "networks of conversations." Therefore, he concludes, "everything human takes place in conversations" (p. 88). In this line of thought, the intimate connection resonates along the history of language, etymologically and biologically speaking.

The understanding of an academic discipline as a conversation resonates with the beginnings of living as humans. We are conversational animals, living beings that live in conversations. As an embodied human activity, conversation reminds us of both the intellectual and emotional aspects of our humanness. We converse with our self as a whole. Truly human conversation requires us to come into it with all our humanness. Therefore, our intellectual systems cannot deny our emotions, even when they no longer rely on spoken language as a way of passing on what is worth conserving. This must have been in Pinar's mind when he uttered his understanding of curriculum as complicated conversation: the emotional aspects of our intellectual undertakings and participation in those socio-intellectual communities named academic fields. Elaborating on this point in *Understanding Curriculum*, Pinar et al. (1995) claim that

> [u]nlike many other textbooks, we wish to preserve the individual voices of individual scholars as much as possible. It seems to us that most textbooks present a field of study as if it were an army of disembodied ideas, marching across the blank space of time, inevitably annexing unincorporated space, establishing cities of systematized thought. The truth is that fields do not proceed that way. Fields are comprised of people, sometimes extraordinary, often ordinary people, whose job is to write material that complies with the rules and principles other people-their predecessors-have established as reasonable. Fields, just like schools, are comprised of people, people with ideas.
>
> (p. 4)

Conversation, therefore, restores academic life as human. A life worth to be lived. Oakeshott (2004) also sees a deep connection between conversation and life. For him, conversation is the best analogy we may find for life. According to him, conversation was initiated "in the primeval forests and extended and made more articulate in the course of the centuries" (Oakeshott, 1991, p. 490). Conversation, he tells us, "springs from the perception of the pleasure of talk" (p. 187), "from the movement of present minds disposed to intellectual adventure" (p. 189). Participating in an academic discipline, joining in that conversation, requires accepting that talk is "to be understood as a partnership in intellectual pleasure" (Oakeshott, 2004, p. 187), a partnership that also requires the acceptance of the ephemerality of our achievements. As a conversation then, any academic discipline can be understood as "an endless unrehearsed intellectual adventure" (Oakeshott, 1989, p. 189). In joining this conversation, a moment and a place for contemplation seems necessary; an "invitation to disentangle oneself, for a time, from the urgencies of the here and now and to listen to the conversation in which human beings forever seek to understand themselves" (Oakeshott, 1989, p. 41)—an initiation through the listening to the various voices without whom a conversation remains impossible. It is in conversation where academic disciplines as human activities find their character. That is why every academic discipline must strive to remain a conversation—a conversation that requires those voices to endure in our human intercourse without being assimilated to each other or to a dominant one. An international conversation must take the form of an intercultural dialogue rather that of a cultural monologue.

Conversation, however, is not only about voices but also about silence. Silence is what makes it possible for the *Otro*'s voice to remain as such, allowing conversation. The listener is a speaker in silence and the speaker a listener *in potentia*. As Benjamin (2004) affirms, "conversation strives toward silence and the listener is really the silent partner" (p. 6). Silence allows listening, *ergo* conversation. The listener then "holds true language in readiness" (Benjamin, 2004, p. 7), speaking a silence that creates the meeting-place of conversation, in Oakeshott's terms. In silence, "energy is renewed, the listener leads the conversation to the age of language, and the speaker creates the silence of a new language, he is first auditor" (Benjamin, 2004, p. 7). Benjamin insists that "silence is the internal frontier of conversation" (2004, p. 7), a border beyond which the *Otro* may be revealed to us as an interpellation. Such a silence then is different from the silence required by a monologue. In a monologue, the speaker is obsessed with the present and he hears only "the rhythm of one's [his] own words in the empty space" (Benjamin, 2004, p. 7). As opposed to monologue, conversation make it possible for "the silent one" to remain as the "unappropriated source of meaning" (Benjamin, 2004, p. 6). Then, and only then, conversation may provide the opportunity of becoming something else, an opportunity for becoming together. That promise awaits in silence in every iteration of human intercourse.

Freire understands very well the need for silence in order to educate for liberation, a silence quite different from the culture of silence he criticizes. His pedagogy is a pedagogy of listening: a listening awaiting the voice of the *Otro* for whom speaking has been denied, his own humanness. Freire expresses this deep conviction in his scholarship, especially in his "spoken books" or "talking books." Those yet useful formulations do not fully convey the meaning of the Portuguese expression *livros conversa* [conversation book]. In one of those *livros conversa*, Freire explains:

> I started doing this with other friends of mine, other educators, in Brazil, maybe five years ago. I called it "spoken books." Instead of writing a book, we speak the book, and afterwards others can transcribe it; but first we have the order of the spoken words. This should give us a duality in the conversation, a certain relaxation, a result of losing seriousness in thinking while talking. The purpose is to have a good conversation but in the sort of style that makes it easier to read the words. In this book we can capture this movement of conversation. The reader goes and comes with the movement of the conversation.
> (Freire & Myles, 1988, p. 4)

The conversation in the book foresees the conversation between the writer and the reader, in the afterlife of the text, as Benjamin would say. The reader then becomes a listener who re-writes the writing, keeping the conversation going. The writer, Freire says, "get[s] to know, to interact with, the distant readers who probably will read the book when he or she is no longer in existence . . ., facing them symbolically" (Freire &

Shor, 1987, p. 2). This ceaseless excavation in the texts is at the center of an intellectual work dealing with the afterlife of texts. Freire's conversational writing is evocative and a fine example of the oral tradition as a "contemplative encounter with the other that reconstructs subjectivity and society" (Pinar, 2012, p. 191). The idea of conversation as human life comes about strongly at a time of global exclusion and planetary agony in which cultural monologue threatens life at its own material level.

According to Pinar (2012), "Oakeshott's characterization of conversation as not conforming to a predetermined end enables us to understand how the aggressive use of standardized examinations cannot countenance a curricular conversation" (p. 193). Therefore, standardized testing, he argues, "destroys those lived links between the spoken word (the classroom by definition is a public sphere) and the inner conversation (carried on in rooms of one's own)" (p. 230). I believe this concern must be located at the center of schooling as a modern educational *dispositif*.[3] Schooling itself is a system of social standardization. This standardization is not unrelated to the process of homogenization begun by Europe at the outset of modernity and whose first subjects were the peoples of *América*. The indigenous people of *Latinoamérica* were the *Otro* whose voices were silenced by Europe's practice of domination. Since that primal experience, *Latinoamérica* was excluded from the conversation of humankind. There was no human encounter but subjugation. There was no conversation but the beginning of a Eurocentric monologue, still at play, that condemns the *Otro*'s voices to silence. Modernity denied the possibility of intercultural dialogue from the beginning. Dussel (1995) writes:

> The inescapable difficulties of such mutual conversation were not even in place, as occurred among the Eurocentric conquistadores. Conversation become impossible, as did any argumentation in a real communication community. . . . [F]rom the moment of Europe's discovery of America, the Europeans disgracefully covered all this over. Under the mantle of forgetfulness and barbaric modernization, Europeans have continued realizing that mythic 1492 throughout the continent.
>
> (p. 87)

Impossibility of conversation during the European invasion of *América*, which I argue is the primal phenomenon of modernity, flowed not from the inescapable difficulty that every conversation entails but from the negation of the *Otro* as a valid interlocutor. The basics of conversation as a human encounter were not even present. Therefore, rather than conversation, what followed 1492 was the deployment of a silencing European cultural monologue. This cultural monologue is still at play in the everyday stronger standardizing global educational policies.

Latinoamérica

América, an island situated between Europe and Asia, was named after a European sailor who partially circumnavigated this "new continent." The act of naming it was made from what Hegel called the heart of Europe, by a German cartographer who baptized the "new continent" "Americo's Land." Until then, this not new but old world, although unknown to the European consciousness, had been imagined by the invaders as a part of Asia. *América* was a European invention, as the Mexican intellectual Edmundo O'Gorman (1995) claims. It was not discovered but un-covered, as Dussel (1995) affirms. Thus, the word *América* in *Latinoamérica* covers up the diversity of cultures existing in *América* before this land was unfairly named as such. *América* has never been named by its proper name. It was a non-being made into being by someone for someone else. For the indigenous peoples of this land, *she*[4] was neither new nor unknown. Leopoldo Zea (1947) affirms that "Latin America is the daughter of European culture; it is the product of one of its major crises. The discovery of *América* was not a matter of chance but rather of necessity" (p. 362). *América* was a promised land for the Europeans. She, *América*, became a future for some other than *her* peoples, peoples that were made into strangers in their own land.[5] The mother was taken over by outsiders that made her their property. For *Mapuche* people, and for the rest of the peoples of the land now called *América*, this land was not a property since they belong to the land and not the other way around. *Mapuche* means people from the land. The people's voices of *América*, before she was so called, were silenced and some of those voices were lost forever in the conversation of humankind.

The word *Latinoamérica* began to be used in the middle of the nineteenth century, some decades after its independence from the Spanish and Portuguese colonial powers. The Chilean intellectual Francisco Bilbao (1866) coined the term *América Latina* in his well-known lecture *Initiative of America: Idea of a Federal Congress of the Republics*, delivered in Paris in June 22, 1856. His intention was to distinguish one América that was *Latina* from the other that was *Anglo-Saxon*. Bilbao called for unity among the republics that had emancipated themselves from the Spanish and Portuguese empires. The term, then, refers to a necessary search for identity as well as autonomy from European and U.S. interferences. Some months later, the Colombian intellectual Torres Caicedo (1866) published his famous poem *Las Dos Américas* [The Two Americas]. The idea was similar to Bilbao's, that there were two *Américas*, one *Anglo-Saxon*, the other, *Latina*. Both Latin American intellectuals published these works in France. The use of the word *Latina* refers to the linguistic identity found in Latin among romance languages. This move also covers up the diversity of languages of the peoples living in this land before the European invasion took place and the Africans enslaved and brought to it during the first centuries of modernity.

Latinoamérica then carries the memory of that moment of liberation that Bilbao and Torres Caicedo sought; it also carries the memory of the negation of the *Otro*. *Latinoamérica* performs the duality of this *mestizo* [mixed race] continent born by the military-erotic-educational European domination started in 1492. In the twentieth century, this memory emerged as a question about the concrete Latin American Being as historically dominated, "the victims of a gigantic cover-up over identity begun on October 12, 1492" (Zea, 1968, p. 372), and continued by the "enlightened" nation states that followed the creation of the European empires. *Latinoamérica* throughout *her* history tended to mirror, adopt, or follow foreign intellectual trends brought from outside even by the insiders. Latin American intellectuals remained Eurocentric. That was inevitable given that there was "no time to originate entire systems. *América*, since gaining her political independence, had never known the *leisure* so necessary for such a creation" (Zea, 1968, p. 4), a reconstructive self-re-creation. However, Zea warns us, "when European thought, of its own accord, leads to historicism, the conscience of America, reflecting this, paradoxically comes face to face with itself; what was reflection becomes auto-reflection" (p. 12). Becoming historical awakened Latin American self-awareness. For the great Mexican intellectual historian Latin America cannot continue being an "echo and shadow" of Europe and its culture, as Hegel claimed in his *Lectures on the Philosophy of World History*, written in the first decades of the nineteenth century. Becoming historical meant to resituate *Latinoamérica* in the world history; it was so for Zea, the thinkers of liberation in the 1960s and 1970s, as it is for us still today. This work of reconstruction, maybe more urgent nowadays, meant also the reconstruction of world history from a planetary horizon.

Yet another *latinoamericano* would add that an authentic Latin American thinking must start by a "meditation *about* our anthropological status and *from* our own negative status, with a view to its cancellation" (Salazar Bondy, 1968, p. 397). In other words, this meditative moment must lead to the negation of the negation of *Latinoamérica* as an oppressed continent. This insight is at the center of the work of the thinkers of liberation from the 1960s and particularly of the philosophy of liberation in the early 1970s. For Latin American societies, the basic dilemma, as formulated by Freire (1965) in the introduction to his *Educación como Práctica de Libertad* [Education as the Practice of Freedom], is "to choose a society partially independent or a society that decolonizes itself more and more, unknotting the ties that made and make it other societies' object" (p. 13).[6] This reconstruction requires a pedagogy of liberation, a pedagogy that enables us to surpass the historical trauma of colonization and slavery and its current instantiations. Reflecting upon this problematic, Enrique Dussel (2011) points out that "American colonization and African slavery have left indelible marks and demand a deep practical and theoretical, ethical, cultural and economic-political transformation of the alterity excluded for centuries" (p. 183). For *Latinoamérica* as a *mestizo* continent, this reconstruction entails the recognition of her *indio* and *negro* heritages. In *Pedagogy of Hope* (1994), Freire recalls a conversation with Eric Fromm in Cuernavaca, Mexico. He writes,

> I hear again in my mind something I once heard from Erich Fromm, in Cuernavaca, Mexico: "this kind of practice", he told me, in our first meeting, arranged by Ivan Illich, at which I had told him how I thought of and practice education, "this kind of educational practice is a kind of historical-cultural, political psychoanalysis."
> (Freire, 1994, p. 55)

That would also be his response to Antonio Faundez in one of his *livros conversa*: "What is needed is a historico-cultural psychoanalysis" (Freire & Faundez, 1989, p. 92). And, then he elaborates, claiming that his pedagogical-political proposal "is a sort of psychoanalysis—an historical, ideological, cultural, political and social psychoanalysis—in which the psychoanalyst couch is replaced by the field of struggle" (Freire & Faundez, 1989, p. 95). It other words, it requires a pedagogy of liberation, which entails both progressive and regressive moments.

The Regressive-Progressive

The words *regressive* and *progressive* describe opposite forces in a field. This opposition is produced by the prefixes *re* and *pro*. The prefix *re* comes from the Latin, meaning back, backward, or again. The prefix *pro* comes from the Greek meaning for, forward, or before. The final part of these two compound words (*gressive*) comes from the Latin *gradi*, meaning to go, to step. Therefore, while the word *regressive* means going backwards, the word *progressive* means going forwards. This temporal movement assumes a given present as the starting point. The idea of a temporal movement as stepping backward or stepping forward seems connected to our metaphorical thinking of time. Lakoff and Johnson (2003) have pointed out that we think of time as a "relative motion with respect to us with the future in front and the past behind" (p. 44). In other words, we conceptualize time "in terms of space" (p. 126) with our body as a present point of reference. This seems to be the way we live time.

This idea of our body as a present point of reference is deeply grounded in our biology. Maturana and Varela (1980) explain that our neuro system "always functions in the present," which "is the interval necessary for an interaction to take place; past, future, and present exist only for the observer" (p. 15). Thus, in the moment of becoming self-conscious we perform a self-observation; "by making descriptions of ourselves (representations), and by interacting with our descriptions we can describe ourselves describing ourselves, in an endless recursive process" (Maturana & Varela,

1980, p. 14). This is why we need to go backwards and forwards seeking for images of ourselves in order to interact with them. We do this with our whole body, as pleasurable and painful as that may be. This autopoietic process restores the present as present and reminds us of ourselves as historical beings. That is why *currere* as a "self-conscious conceptualization of the temporal" and "what is conceptualized through time" (Pinar, 1976, p. 51) allows subjective and social reconstruction by "transcending the given toward the field of possibles" (Sartre, 1963, p. 93).

According to Sartre (1963), "the regressive-progressive method takes into account *at the same time* the circularity of the material conditions and the mutual conditioning of the human relations established on that basis" (p. 75). To him, the regressive (Psychoanalysis) and the progressive (Marxism) informed his *Search for a Method* (1963). The existentialist method is "at once both regressive and progressive" (Sartre, 1963, p. 133). Sartre goes on to say "we define a double simultaneous relationship. In relation to the given, the *praxis* is negativity" but in relation to the desired, the future, that "praxis is positivity, but this positivity opens onto the 'non-existent,' " (p. 92) toward what has not yet been.

The words *regressive* and *progressive* are also used to convey the meaning of something threatening or favorable to human life. A *regressive* policy or a *regressive* period of history is a policy or period of history that threatens life, such as the imperialistic policy of the Nazi period in Germany. And a *progressive* policy or period is one that favors life, such as the abolition of slavery or the liberation movements in the 1960s. There are probably biological and cultural reasons for this value-laden relation with past and future. The positive connotation of the progressive is connected with the idea of future—perhaps because it means to prevail, to endure. The project "orients life" (Sartre, 1963, p. 108).

In cultural terms, the progressive is probably connected with our conception of progress, as problematic as that may be. Again the conversation takes us to the center of modernity and the narrative of progress. Benjamin's (1968) insight is helpful. He writes, "there is no document of civilization that is not at the same time a document of barbarism" (p. 256). *Thanatos* and *Eros* are acting forces in our past, present, and future life. The moment of comprehension must be then "simultaneously progressive (toward the objective result) and regressive (I go back to the original condition)" (Sartre, 1963, p. 154). In other words, the temporal complexity introduced by this past-looking and future-looking movement enables understanding as well as reconstruction. Benjamin insists that thought dialectically influences every historical moment becomes "a force field (*Kraftfeld*) in which the conflict between fore-and afterhistory plays itself out. It becomes that field as it is penetrated by actuality" (quoted in Jay, 1993, p. 3). In the interplay of past and future, the present becomes historical. This working through the past, seeking for the future, requires "a willingness to intervene destructively as well as constructively" (Jay, 1993, p. 1); it requires the destruction of the whole (analysis) in order to construct a new moment of unity (synthesis).

The Analytical-Synthetical

Like the *regressive-progressive* pair, the *analytical-synthetical* also carries opposite meanings. In contrast, however, this time naming the movement is more difficult. It is not an inside-outside dynamic but implies the taking apart of elements that compound a unity. In this force field we find centrifugal-centripetal forces. We allow a temporal loss of unity (analysis) before re-unification (synthesis). *Analytical* derives *from analysis*, which is composed of the Greek verb *analy*—to loosen up and the Greek suffix *sis* which denotes action. The *analytical* entails the meaning of losing unity. The *synthetical* comes from synthesis which is composed of the Greek prefix *syn*—with, together, and *tithénai*—to put, to place. Again, *sis* denoting action, makes the *synthetical* convey the meaning of putting something together. That is, what analysis separates, synthesis puts together again. We lose ourselves in order to find ourselves. Destruction precedes reconstruction.

Maturana and Varela (1980) claim that as human beings we inherit world views that consist of parts put together. Those superimposed significations "are isolated and enumerated by analysis. The movement that joins them together *in life* is, on the contrary, synthetic" (Sartre, 1963, p. 108). Historically, "synthesis seems to have been too much for the human mind—where practical affairs were concerned" (Maturana & Varela, 1980, p. 63). Nevertheless, a momentary synthesis seems desirable after a period of intensive thinking, such as a doctoral experience. The analytical tendency to study each tradition in its distinctiveness is in tension with the tendency to think between and beyond each tradition. Methodologically, in this work synthesis is driven by the logic of analogy rather of identity. In other words, it relies on the project of an intercultural dialogue that may inform education as human in the only planet we inhabit.

Talking From the South

Talking from the South means choosing a *locus enunciationis* which has historically been the place of reception of others' discourses. This does not mean that there were no southern voices millennia before Europe become the center of a world-system that progressively made the rest of the world its periphery. And it does not mean that there have not been utterances talking back to that process from the underside of history during the five centuries that that process has lasted. Those voices, however, have been either ignored or subsumed into the discourses of the center, whose Eurocentric echoes are still heard across the present Global South. To make the claim that any scholarship has the South as its *locus enuntiationis* is to say that we are thinking beyond Eurocentrism, meaning thinking at a planetary level, not from provincial Europe and the United States.

Latin American voices are part of the Global South that has historically resisted what Boaventura de Sousa Santos (2014) calls epistemic genocide. This awareness was aroused in *Latinoamérica* during the second half of the twentieth century. The process of epistemological *conscientizacao* led to what we now know as the decolonizing turn: announced in the middle of the past century, articulated in the late 1960s and early 1970s, and matured in the 1990s. At that point it became evident that decolonizing meant to take the point of view of the rejected part of the dual being that our *Latinoamérica mestiza* is. This is the point of view of the stubbornly alive *indio* peoples of *América* that condemned the celebration of 500 years of the Discovery of *América* and called for commemoration of 500 years of resistance. That was the Other's interpellation that was heard in 1992.

Responding to that interpellation, I decided to talk from the South, that epistemological and geographical place to which I belong. I wished to listen to voices of the *indios* of the Global South, specifically to the more southern people in the world, those that inhabited the most southern land of my *América mestiza*. Those people are the *Selknam* or *Onas*, also called *Fueguinos*, given its location in *Tierra del Fuego* [Land of Fire]. They were able to inhabit one of the most difficult landscapes in Earth. They survived and prospered in spite of the hardship of the environment but they did not survive the human hunt that the nation states of Argentina and Chile, alongside with their European newcomers and helpers, launched onto them. This genocide took place between the second half of the nineteenth century and the first decades of the twentieth. That is the same time that the colonial order was established in Asia, Africa, and Oceania. The genocide of the *Selknam* people continued the process begun by the Spanish Empire at the outset of modernity. I cannot listen to their voices, because they are gone. Silence reigns uninterrupted in those landscapes. In the margins of the margins, the peripheries of the periphery, death was the destiny pronounced on those peoples. I am leaving this theoretical *détente* listening to the voices already gone. I listen to the silence. I honor the absence of their bodies from which no voice can come. Utterance supposes "aliveness." This is a materialism which is older than the old one and more spiritual than the new one.

Notes

1. I am borrowing this expression from Dr. Cristal Tomas (2014) whose dissertation work I knew through her presentation in Dr. McCarthy's pre-seminar on *Cultural Studies and Critical Interpretations*, a required course of the *Concentration in Cultural Studies and Interpretative Methodologies* that I took as part of my doctoral program. She explains that taking on "a phenomenological or philosophical attitude" is useful because it provides a *détente*, an analytical pause (though one not absent of tension), in which the surfaces of things and the common sense notions we have about things can be separated.

2. The conception of theory as a process of cultivation of the person has become apocryphal. Today it appears to us that the mimetic conformity of the soul to the proportions of the universe, which seemed accessible to contemplation, had only taken theoretical knowledge into the service of the internationalization of norms and thus estranged it from its legitimate task. (Habermas, 1971, p. 304)
3. I am using this term, usually translated into English as *apparatus*, in its Foucauldian sense. This term, for Agamben (2009) is a *terminus technicus* in Foucault's work, which he understands as a "sort of—shall we say—formation which has as its major function at a given historical moment that of responding to an urgent need. The apparatus thus has a dominant strategic function. This may have been, for example, the assimilation of a floating population found to be burdensome for an essentially mercantilist economy: there was a strategic imperative acting here as the matrix for an apparatus which gradually undertook the control or subjection of madness, sexual illness and neurosis." (Foucault, 1977 in Agamben, 2009, p. 2)
4. In Spanish language, where nouns carry gender, *América* as a noun is feminine.
5. Having biblical resonances, this expression was also used by Fanon in his work. He writes: "at the moment when the nationalist parties are mobilizing the people in the name of national independence, the native intellectual sometimes spurns these acquisitions which he suddenly feels make him a stranger in his own land" (Fanon, 2004, p. 219).
6. Free translation.

References

Agamben, G. (2009). *"What is an apparatus?" and other essays.* Berkeley, CA: Stanford University Press.
Benjamin, W. (2004). Goethe's elective affinities. In M. P. Bullock & M. W. Jennings (Eds.) (1996–2002). *Walter Benjamin: Selected writings, Volume 1 1913–1926* (pp. 297–360). Cambridge, MS: Harvard University Press.
Benjamin, W. (1968). *Illuminations.* New York, NY: Schocken Books.
Bilbao, F. (1866). *Obras completas de Francisco Bilbao.* Buenos Aires: Imprenta Buenos Aires.
De Sousa Santos, B. (2014). *Epistemologies of the South: Justice against epistemicide.* London: Routledge.
Dussel, E. (2011). *Politics of liberation: A critical world history.* London: SCM Press.
Dussel, E. (1995). *The invention of the Americas: Eclipse of "the other" and the myth of modernity.* New York, NY: Continuum.
Fanon, F. (2004). *The wretched of the earth.* New York, NY: Grove Press.
Freire, P. (1994). *Pedagogy of hope: Reliving pedagogy of the oppressed.* New York, NY: Continuum.
Freire, P. (1965). *La educación como práctica de la libertad.* Santiago de Chile: ICIRA.
Freire, P., & Faundez, A. (1989). *Learning to question: A pedagogy of liberation.* Geneva: World Council of Churches.
Freire, P., & Myles, H. (1988). *We make the road by walking: Conversations on education and social change.* Philadelphia, PA: Temple University Press.
Freire, P., & Shor, I. (1987). *A pedagogy for liberation: Dialogues on transforming.* South Hadley, MA: Bergin & Garvey Publishers.
Habermas, J. (1971). *Knowledge and human interests.* Boston, MA: Beacon Press.

Jay, M. (1993). *Force fields: Between intellectual history and cultural critique.* New York, NY: Routledge.

Jay, M. (1984). *Adorno.* Cambridge, MA: Harvard University Press.

Kuhn, T. S. (1962). *The structure of scientific revolutions* (1st ed.). Chicago, IL: University of Chicago Press.

Lakatos, I. (1978). *The methodology of scientific research programmes: Philosophical papers volume 1.* Cambridge: Cambridge University Press.

Lakoff, G., & Johnson, M. (2003). *Metaphors we live by.* Chicago, IL: University of Chicago Press.

Laudan, L. (1977). *Progress and its problems.* Berkeley, CA: University of California Press.

Maturana, H. (2008). *The origin of humanness in the biology of love.* Exeter: Imprint Academic.

Maturana, H., & Varela, F. (1980). *Autopoiesis and cognition: The realization of the living.* Dordrecht, Holland: D. Reidel Publishing Company.

Miller, J. (2009). Curriculum studies and transnational flows and mobilities: Feminist autobiographical perspectives. In E. Ropo & T. Autio (Eds.). *International conversations on curriculum studies: Subject, society and curriculum* (pp. 43–70). Rotterdam: Sense Publishers.

Oakeshott, M. (2004). The voice of conversation in the education of mankind. In L. O'Sullivan (Ed.). *What is history? And other essays.* Charlottesville, VA: Imprint Academic.

Oakeshott, M. (1991). The voice of poetry in the conversation of mankind. In M. Oakeshott. *Rationalism in politics and other essays.* Indianapolis, IN: Liberty Press.

Oakeshott, M. (1989). *The voice of liberal learning.* New Haven, CN: Yale University Press.

O'Gorman, E. (1995). *La invención de América.* México: Fondo de Cultura Económica.

Pinar, W. F. (2015). *Educational experience as lived: Knowledge, history, alterity.* New York, NY: Palgrave Macmillan.

Pinar, W. F. (2012). *What is curriculum theory?* New York, NY: Routledge.

Pinar, W. F. (2011). *The character of curriculum studies: Bildung, currere, and the recurring question of the subject.* New York, NY: Palgrave Macmillan.

Pinar, W. F. (1976). Self and others. In W. F. Pinar & M. R. Grumet. *Toward a poor curriculum* (pp. 7–30). Dubuque, IA: Kendall/Hunt.

Pinar, W. F., & Grumet, M. (1976). *Toward a poor curriculum.* Dubuque, IA: Kendall/Hunt.

Pinar, W. F., Reynolds, W. M., Slattery, P., & Taubman, P. M. (Eds.) (1995). *Understanding curriculum: An introduction to the study of historical and contemporary curriculum discourses.* New York, NY: Peter Lang.

Salazar Bondy, A. (1968). *¿Existe una filosofía en nuestra América?* México: Siglo XXI.

Sartre, J. P. (1963). *Search for a method.* New York, NY: Knopf.

Zea, L. (1968). *Antología de la filosofía americana contemporánea.* México: Costa AMIC.

Zea, L. (1947). *Ensayos sobre filosofía en la historia.* México: Stylo.

3 The Regressive-Progressive

I start this chapter by describing my current biographical-historical situation in which this study is grounded. I describe the present as *given* and the project with which the process of becoming historical begins. I live this present as a *given*, as a time for my study of the study of educational experience, a time that must include a reflection on the current situation of the field of curriculum and education in general in the global context of the second decade of the twenty-first century, when curriculum struggles to remain conversation (Pinar, 2012) in the midst of a global deployment of a culture of silence. This present begins also with the time when a new generation in Chile is starting its struggle for a better education for all. In a time when any future that is not the repetition of the same seemed impossible, a new generation of Chilean students rejected that as a present. The 2011 student protests[1] in Chile resonate with that past, with my past, my present, screaming future.

Situating my narrative in such a present, marked by a paralyzing attitude that talks about the impossibility of another future, I look backward to the 1960s as a regressive time when the technological conception of education was overwhelmingly deployed through the arriving of the field of curriculum into Latin America. I look backward to the prehistory of my life, the historical given in which I came into life. In that also presentistic present, the regressive 1960s, I found the first talking back to that instrumental educational rationality both in Latin America and shortly after in the United States. I began my schooling during the 1970s, what 1960 had left for us.

I was born at 5:30 AM on November 12, 1969. It was a difficult birth. First, I was not in the right position, and then my head was too big, which made the birth giving work painful and frighteningly dangerous. There was risk of neonatal asphyxia. My mom rejected the doctor's intentions of using an iron tool to take me out. She was afraid of a possible deformation from the pressure put upon my head by the instrument. That made things even more difficult, but she made it and I was brought into life, into a world. Sooner than later, my Aunt Lucy came; she was the first person, other than my parents Silvia and Pedro, to see me. I smiled at her, I was told. Then, Julio and Eliana came and they became my godparents. As traumatic as my birth was, I was received into a world of plentiful love.

Remembering the Present

Remembering the present as present means to become historical. A presentistic attitude to the present is ahistorical. The present belongs in relation to—is wedged in-between—the past and the future. Historical consciousness requires attentiveness to the temporal complexity and structure of human existence. As Freire affirms in his *Pedagogy of the Oppressed* (1970a), rather than being alive,[2] human beings exist, and "their existence is historical" (p. 98). Speaking in intellectual syntony with the existential tradition, Freire insists that in a context where human beings' historicity is denied, women and men are "divided between an identical past and present, and a future without hope" (Freire, 1970a, p. 173); "transformation occurs in their own existential time, never outside it" (Freire, 1970a, p. 16). It is in that "existential time" where men and women find themselves as historical being, that they are able to make history. Freire reminds us that the present time is just present, a space for practicing freedom; it is the space for our historical consciousness to be cultivated. This cultivation entails the need to look to the past, to the future, to the present of our history; to look within and without. I begin by remembering my present, my existential situation. Having had to live life looking forward, as Kierkegaard famously said, I stop to look backward, activating the past in my present and seeking to make sense of it.

A Fulbright scholarship to study for a Ph.D. in the United States brought my *mestizo* body first to New York, for a couple of days; then to Louisiana, for a couple of months; and, then to Illinois for several years. An unexpected journey for one whose existence had been located and lived beyond the explained variance and mathematical hope of educational achievement. It was not my parents' case, for whom the only possible heritage to leave us was education.

> Abandoned by her husband, my grandmother left the countryside with her two daughters to go to *Concepcion*. She and my aunt worked washing other people's clothes, as *lavanderas*, while sending my mother to school. I don't know how much schooling my grandma had I think she could read; I know my Aunt Lucy attended school for some years, but she was the oldest, so she was the one who had to work. My mother finished primary school; she was a great student but she could not continue studying, she had to work. She told me once she thought about studying a couple of years more, so she could become a teacher, which was possible at that time when there were not too many teachers in Chile and the school system was growing. But she had to work.
>
> (Johnson-Mardones, 2014, p. 250)

Serendipitously, or not, this coming to study the Anglo-Saxon tradition of curriculum sent me back to my own educational tradition. It was first the news of the Chilean student movement in 2011 shown every day on the Facebook wall that somehow forced me to dig into my decision to leave Chile to study and the nature of that experience. It was also listening to my friend Sari speaking with such passion of Paulo Freire during our first doctoral meetings that complicated, and enriched my thoughts. We were in the United States, she was from Indonesia, I from Chile, Freire from Brazil, and the conversation was taking place in English. Marilyn's question about the difference between life history and narrative inquiry raised in her class on teacher education research led me back to the modernity-postmodernity debate during the 1990s, and it made possible a connection with my study of beginning history teacher's identity in Chile. That had been the topic of my master's thesis at the Universidad de Chile in Santiago. It was a thesis that one night made me cry:

> That night, I realized that I had written my own story. Better, I had found my own story in their stories. There was a "we" there, the history of the poor people in Chile; a nonofficial history, non-taught history, unwritten history. Stories told just a couple of times, by us or for us; some of them told only once. That night, I asked myself the same question over and over: Why me? How was this even possible? I recalled my parents, my childhood, our house, the school; memories of that other country, that other Chile, those other Chiles.
> (Johnson-Mardones, 2014, p. 249)

I cannot avoid thinking as I write these lines that the only thing strong enough to push me to abandon my southern home in Concepcion, first to Santiago and then to Urbana-Champaign, was my desire to study. Later, I would become aware of the many resonances that those experiences opened during my first years of doctoral studies. The Facebook walls that disseminated the Chilean student movement all over the globe made me think of the walls of *Latinoamérica's* streets that in the 1960s carried the political-artistic works of a generation committed to social change, the walls that supported the works of the *muralistas mexicanos* [Mexican muralists] that pictured *Latinoamérica* as *mestiza* during the decades that followed the *revolución Mexicana* [Mexican revolution], the walls that screamed freedom during the struggle against the dictatorship in the 1970s and 1980s, the walls that separate borders in the pitiful attempt of the powerful to avoid the mobility of bodies to ensure the mobility of their capitals, the wall hung with the paintings that I already missed so much along with the friends that painted them. Even later, I would become aware that resonances are made possible by those walls—a thought that came to me through the study of biographical approaches in education and qualitative inquiry where the concept of narrative resonance is alluded to, though not quite developed. My intuition was, still is, that the idea of narrative resonance enables one to move from the idea of inquiry and the Eurocentric gaze, characteristic of the academic disciplines, to the space of listening, that allows one to move beyond Eurocentrism. It is true that I kept the word theory in the title of my second chapter, but I must clarify that I imagine that word beyond the Western ocularcentrism of which Martin Jay speaks, as my friend Mike (Dr. Michael Parsons) does not fail to remind me while commenting on my writings. In fact, using the metaphor of words as a gravitational center in constellations of intellectual influences permitted me to move the conversation beyond Eurocentrism and its foundational Hellenocentrism. That move was also made possible by my study of the scholarship of Walter Benjamin for whom words were walls that hide our true content, consistently using a story from the Torah, as Scholem (1981) reminds us in his *Walter Benjamin: A History of a Friendship*. It is through words as material content that we can perform our search for true content; after all we can only see the walls. Everything else sounds to me too pretentious. At least "screaming meanings" towards those words-as-walls, some resonances may be heard. As I said before, my search is dialogical—through words—and not fully conceptual.

Interpellated by the student movement in the South while self-displaced in the North, I became more aware of the presence of the two educational traditions colliding in my doctoral experience—the Anglo-Saxon and the *latinoamericana*. The duality informing that process resonated in the duality of my *mestizo* body, which at some point during these years became the primal image of my reflection. Benjamin (2004) insists that thought dialectically influences every historical moment and becomes a force field (*Kraftfeld*) in which the conflict between fore-and after-history plays itself out. The use of the *mestizo latinoamericano* as a dialectical image (Benjamin, 2008, 2004, 1999, 1968) informed by the use of allegory—connecting two historical experiences—allows me to connect the colonizing arrival of Curriculum Studies as a technological approach to education in *Latinoamérica* in the 1960s and 1970s with the beginning of modernity and the problem of colonialism. This *regressive* moment (Denzin, 1989, 2013a, 2013b; Sartre, 1963) reenacts the European invasion of *América* more than 500 years ago. The *progressive* moment (Denzin, 1989, 2013a, 2013b; Sartre, 1963) reveals itself in the call of the surviving indigenous communities in 1992 to commemorate 500 years of resistance instead of the so-called "discovery." I hope to use the *mestizo* as a dialectical image, as an object of analysis "uniquely capable of producing kinds of meaning that are otherwise inaccessible or unrepresentable" (Jennings and Doherty in Benjamin, 2008, p. 169). The *mestizo latinoamericanos* live their lives in a force field of regressive and progressive impulses.

This intuition of drawing on the idea of dialectical image and specifically of the *mestizo latinoamericano* as dialectical images has proved fruitful. Using the metaphor of force field (Jay, 1993), I may say that the *mestizo latinoamericano* as modernity's dialectical image becomes a starry shining point in the darkness. As suggestive as it is already, it is only after careful contemplation that one realizes that it is not one point but many. Then, one becomes aware of this dialectical image's powerful gravitational attraction around which a constellation may be found. The constellation's first component is its center, the word *mestizo latinoamericano*. Different intellectual traditions gravitate around this center or visible distant point. This center of attraction takes us to the body, since the *mestizo latinoamericano* lives modernity's contradictions in his and her own body. Therefore, it situates our reflection at a material level. In addition, this gravitational center addresses the idea of race in an intellectual context that has historically and systematically negated the category of race in the study of Latin American societies. However, a thorough study of the *mestizo latinoamericano* as modernity's dialectical image requires the study of images that image it. Those images are to be found in a variety of sources and formats such as narrative, painting, poetry, new papers, letters, official documents, buildings, essays, etc. This exceeds the focus of this work, but requires at least an impressionistic address.

The *Mestizo Latinoamericano* as a Dialectical Image

According to Walter Benjamin, history breaks down not into stories but into images, images that according to him come through words. His study of high capitalism or *Le Modernite* focuses on specific images he found in literary works. To Benjamin, the images that allow us to delve into the meaning of modernity are, for instance, the *flâneur* and the prostitute of Parisian arcades. Without fully abandoning a Eurocentric perspective, Benjamin conceptualizes his object of study as high capitalism, which he uses indistinguishably with the term modernity. This, perhaps unintended, intuition opens the space to move our reflection to a non-Eurocentric perspective, and to look at the previous centuries that built the high capitalism or *mature* modernity that Benjamin's dialectical images portray (Benjamin; 2008, 2004, 1999, 1968). To Benjamin, these "figures of thought" or "dialectical images" are the analytical objects in which the spirit of an epoch can be grasped. This is a sort of Freirean codification in which a theme of an epoch can be seen as the "concrete representation of many of these ideas, values, concepts, and hopes, as well as the obstacles which impede the people's full humanization" (Freire, 1970a, p. 101). A dialectical image makes visible a primal phenomenon in history. Therefore, forging a non-Eurocentric understanding of modernity, questioning the self-definition of modernity as just a self-determined phenomenon, re-queries a planetary point of view that resituates the beginning of modernity—namely situating its beginning around the turning of the sixteenth century.

> The birthday of modernity is 1492, even though its gestation, like that of the fetus, required a period of intrauterine growth. Whereas

modernity gestated in the free, creative European cities, it came to birth in Europe's confrontation with the other. By controlling, conquering, and violating the Other, Europe defined itself as discoverer, conquistador and colonizer of an alterity likewise constitutive of modernity. Europe never discovered (*des-cubierto*) this Other as Other but covered over (*encubierto*) the other as part of the Same: i.e. Europe.

(Dussel, 1995, p. 12)

I seek for an image to think modernity from that point of view. I believe that from a worldwide perspective, modernity's dialectical image is the *mestizo latinoamericano*. As such it becomes the gravitational center of a force field of a primal phenomenon. That primal phenomenon is the invasion of a continent—a World Island located between Asia and Europe. This is the primal phenomenon of that historical period called modernity. The *mestizo latinoamericano* is the primal image of the primal history of modernity. Through its study it may be possible to unfold the first and deepest sources of the self *latinoamericano* as well as of modernity.

Therefore, drawing on Benjamin's idea of dialectical image, this work reflects on the concept of modernity in the context of world history. This means to go beyond the still pervasive Eurocentric definition of modernity. It means that instead of looking for modernity's dialectical image in the Europe of the eighteenth or nineteenth centuries, we need to do it from the sixteenth century in *América*. Then the phenomenon of modernity is seen at a planetary scale. Within this non-Eurocentric perspective, the *mestizo latinoamericano* emerges as modernity's dialectical image. The *mestizo* carries in his body the trauma of conquest and slavery, the two historical processes at the base of modernity as a worldwide phenomenon, the two first "holocausts" for which modern Europe is responsible. As Dussel (1995, 1996) has suggested, the *mestizo latinoamericano* is the only race as old as modernity. The conquest of *América* was not just a politico-military-economic undertaking but it was also a process of erotic domination of the *Indias Occidentales* [Western Indias], as the Spaniards called this not-new continent. Through that process, a hybrid being was brought into life. I argue that the *mestizo latinoamericano* is the true dialectical image of modernity understood from a planetary horizon.

Focusing on this entity, it may be possible to unpack the meaning of a historical process that, centuries after this initial moment, has developed into today's global situation. *América*, according to Anibal Quijano (2008), was constituted "as the first space/time of a new model of power of global vocation" (p. 533) that connected the idea of race and colonialism. To Quijano, "the idea of race was a way of granting legitimacy to the relations of domination imposed by the conquest" (p. 535). The *mestizo* is a race brought into life alongside modernity, Europe becoming a center of the world-system by making *América* into its first periphery. This process was already present in the naming of this unknown world.

Explaining what he sees as the weak character of the *latinoamericano*, Octavio Paz (1961) in his *El Laberinto de la Soledad* [Labyrinth of Solitude], refers to this Latin American being in his chapter entitled *Los hijos de la Chingada*. Literally, the expression means children of a raped woman. Thus, as *hijos de la Malinche* [Malinche's children], the *mestizo latinoamericano* are the children of a historical rape that took place in the underside of modernity. The *mestizo latinoamericano* is the child of modernity. This association of *Latinoamérica*, as a *mestizo* continent, with the Malinche is a part of both popular and "high" culture in Latin America. The first *mestizo* is Martín Cortez, illegitimate son of Hernán Cortez and Malinche, an Indian young woman given to Cortez. Malinche, the *india* mother, and Cortez, the European father, are the symbolic originary couple of the *mestizo latinoamericano*.

This symbolism explains the main role that the couple has in Mexican muralism, for instance. Rivera and Orozco made these progenitors some of the main characters of their works. It is Jorge González Camarena, however, who explicitly used the term *pareja original* [original couple] to name the Spanish soldier and Native woman that gave birth to the *mestizo* race. The original couple is part of the famous *mural* that the Mexican artist painted in the *Casa del Arte* [House of the Arts] in the University of Concepción. Painted between 1964 and 1965, the *mural* is entitled *Presencia de América Latina* [Presence of Latin American]. Camarena's original couple resonates with Malinche and Cortez as originary symbolic elements of the primal phenomenon of modernity. The *indio* and the *español* are the originary components of the dialectical image of modernity: the *mestizo* is the product of the erotic domination of *América*.

The *mestizo latinoamericano* is an orphan child before his own father who makes him an object of his pedagogical domination. His pedagogy seeks to make sure that her barbarian heritage remains forgotten. The *mestizo latinoamericano* is a child that needs to be educated, a barbarian that needs domination to reach the gift of civilization. He is the child-son-disciple who never rises to the same level as his father-adult-educator. In this situation the disciple must remain silent before his preceptor. This is the pedagogical deployment of what Freire called the culture of silence. It is the silence in which the survival cultures have been kept, first by the empire and then by the nation state. It is also the silence in which the *mestizo* has to keep his mother's culture, collectively and individually.

Together with the erotic process of domination by the *conquistador* over the *india* and the political process of European domination over the *indio* and the *negro*, pedagogical domination begins with the indoctrination that follows the conquest. As we may see, modernity is also a pedagogical project whose deployment over *Latinoamérica* differs enormously from the educational ideal formulated during the enlightenment.

The educational formulation of modernity and its institutionalization in the so-called modern educational system is also informed by the historical dynamics underlying the constitution of Europe as a center of the world-system. This pedagogy is part of modern ontology since the European father constitutes his *mestizo* son or daughter into a depository of his will of power. The pedagogy of modernity is a pedagogy of domination that follows and reenacts the political-military and erotic "colonization of the indigenous life-world (*Lebenswelt*)" (Dussel, 1995, p. 46).

Therefore, the image of the *mestizo latinoamericano*, as it is used here, opens up an interpretative space to unfold the complexities and complications involved in the construction of an academic discipline as a worldwide field aiming at decolonization. This aim entails the necessity of working through the past. As a dual being, the *mestizo latinoamericano* struggles between his father's and his mother's heritage: the European conqueror and the conquered *indio*, the colonizer and the colonized, the oppressor and the oppressed (Fanon, 2004, 1967; Freire, 1970a; Memmi, 1974). It was the rejected part of his identity that shows itself alive in the *indio*'s speaking up of 1992. It is this element that needs to be acknowledged and which requires reconstruction in order to surpass the historical trauma of the conquest. The reconstruction of himself and herself in order to find synthesis requires a pedagogy of liberation.

The Regressive 1960s and the Culture of Silence

The 1960s, the Prehistory of My Life

I heard of that time from my parents and other loved ones. It was a time when everything seemed to be possible. It was the time my parents fell in love, got married, and eventually begot me. It was a time of life and love, of youth and courage. It was the time of May 1968, when people were realistic by asking for the impossible, and not only in France.

> In 1968, Italian workers and students joined in solidarity to strike to improve working conditions and conditions in schools. Women also struck and protested, demanding equal pay. A series of occupations and protests led by intellectuals such as Antonio Negri, Oreste Scalzone, and Franco Piperno on university and high school campuses, called for not only more responsive educational institutions but a curriculum that represented Italy's colonial and Fascist past in terms of class conflict. Italy as an *idea* infused with images of imperial power and splendor and deployed to strengthen the state emerged as secondary to the economic dynamics structuring the daily lives of workers and students.
>
> (Salvio, 2014, p. 272)

It was the time of the agrarian reform, the educational reform, the reform of Chilean universities, the red universities in the Americas as my friend Tata calls them, the time when songs still alive were composed, the time of the flower revolution, the time of the Second Vatican Council and the time of the Latin American Bishops Conference in Medellin, Colombia, the time of the civil rights movement in the United States, Prague's Spring, and so on. It was even the time when Chile won the third place in World Cup soccer. The 1960s were good times. But they were other times. They were times quite different from the 1970s when I lived my early childhood under Pinochet's dictatorship—a time when nothing was possible.

The 1960s, the Prehistory of My Life

I will read them against the grain as a regressive time in history. It was a time when the U.S. intervention in *Latinoamérica* increased, securing American interests in *Latinoamérica*, expressed dramatically in its support of military coups that began in 1964 in Brazil and reached Chile in 1973. It was the time of Kennedy's assassination. It was the time of the Vietnam War, the time of the death of heroes of the counter culture in the United States and the assassination of the black movement's leaders, the time of the assassination of Lumumba in Congo, the time of the Algeria War. The 1960s were violent times. It was the time of the *Tlatelolco Massacre*,[3] and it was also the time when the field of curriculum made its way into *Latinoamérica*. This experience of the 1960s is fundamental not just for the generation of scholars that lived it as adults or young adults but also for the next generation born around the end of the decade. The year 1968 remains an epiphanic moment.

Díaz-Barriga and García-Garduño say about the Mexican context:

> As it has been studied by several authors (Díaz-Barriga, 2011; Glazman, 2011), the entry of the field of curriculum in Mexico had a lot to do with the social conditions that prevailed in that epoch. The student movement of 1968, in which thousands of university students lost their lives, brought along an opening process that eroded the rigid and authoritarian structure of the *Priista*[4] regime. The new *Priista* regime wanted reconciliation with the demands of the population by a relative democratic openness.
>
> (2014, p. 242)

In her "Footprints and Marks on the Intellectual History of Curriculum Studies in Mexico," Alicia De Alba (2011) writes:

> I belong to that generation of 1968, like in France; in Mexico there was also a student movement that marked the generation 1968 and the following generations. Within the frame of this movement and with

> the zeal of achieving successful Olympic Games, we have in our history the genocide committed by the government on October 2 1968, where they assassinated, with impunity, a great number of students. That day I was not at the meeting but the events of 1968 marked me, like they marked the majority of those of us that were students at that time.
>
> (p. 50)

"Nineteen sixty-eight was a violent year, indeed" (Pinar, 2015, p. 3). The violence of the 1960s was the answer to what Freire called the "culture of silence" of those who, rejecting a deadly present, dared to speak of a future. The biographical and historical experience of the violence in the 1960s, expressed in torture, exile, assassination, and military coups, resonate with the historical trauma in the *longue durée* history of *Latinoamérica*, the traumas of conquest and slavery. The latter speaks of modernity in the long run, while the former, the 1960s, speaks of modernization of the under-developed world during the past century. That is the context in which Curriculum Studies crossed the *Rio Bravo*.

The Arrival of Curriculum Studies in *Latinoamérica*

Chile is an intriguing case study in the history of the field of curriculum in *Latinoamérica*. Chile had attracted international attention with a series of utopian projects that characterized its history during the 1960s. The country was designated a "'showcase' for the Alliance for Progress—a United States effort to stave off revolutionary movements in Latin America by bolstering centrist, middle-class, Christian Democratic political parties" (Kornbluh, 2003, p. xiii). As Zemelman and Jara (2006) affirm, without abandoning its interventionist approach, the United States favored centrist governments that endorsed the U.S. democratic model as a way to prevent another Cuban revolution in the continent. Hence, the United States distanced itself from its traditional oligarchical allies and right-wing parties. Alliance for Progress was the new U.S. strategy in the region, though not the only one. Alliance for Progress was launched in the Extraordinary Meeting of the Inter-American Economic and Social Council in 1961 in Punta del Este, Uruguay, two years after the Cuban Revolution in 1959, and it contained an agenda in which education was a main element. In one of the annexed resolutions, the Punta del Este agreement encouraged Latin American countries to "adopt an integral plan of education, in order to elevate the cultural level of their peoples, which it must concord with the other reforms recommended by the Alliance" (Zemelman & Jara, 2006, p. 116). The following year a Commission for the Integral Planning of Education was created in Chile.

The basic elements of that agenda matched the program of Eduardo Frei, a Christian Democrat politician who was elected President in 1964 with the largest margin in Chilean electoral history. An important factor in that was the U.S. support of Frei's campaign. This support was not only in the way of the Alliance for Progress package but also in specific interventions documented in the *Covert Action in Chile 1963–1973* and *Alleged Assassination Plots Involving Foreign Leaders*, which detailed several operations, including the U.S. government's covert campaign in Chile. These documents were the result of the first U.S. Congress investigation into clandestine operations. Based on this and other declassified files, Kornbluh (2003) comments that the "CIA would subsequently credit these covert operations with helping Frei to an overwhelming 57 percent majority victory on September 4, 1964—a margin unheard of in Chile's typical three-way presidential races" (p. 5). Clearly, the arrival of the Anglo-Saxon field of curriculum in *Latinoamérica* was marked by increasing U.S. intervention.

The educational reform of 1965 was influenced by this continental agenda stimulated by the Cold War rationale. It is important to note that much of the "human capital" that would participate in the reform had been educated abroad during the last part of the previous decade and the beginning of the one in which the reform took place. This was also connected to international assistance programs. Following Schiefelbein (1976), Fischer (1979) comments that one of the outcomes of this assistance was "highly skilled educational planners and economists who returned to Chile from studies abroad, bringing with them a new level of educational technology and research methodology" (p. 38). The faith that this intelligentsia shared was that education was a tool for development "that could be sharpened and refined to work more efficiently and effectively" (Fischer, 1979, p. 55). Frei's educational reform had a broader framework of theories of development and modernization, where the main role of education was to contribute to the economic growth of the country. Ruiz (2010) says that in

> this perspective marked by theories of human capital and by Schultz's studies of the economic value of education, Frei's Minister of Education, Juan Gómez Millas, remembers in his discourse that education, which was traditionally considered a luxury and a way of consumption, "is today regarded as consumption-investment. As investment it is has the highest economic performance and its right administration is decisive to all fundamental aspects of human development."
>
> (p. 91)[5]

Education and economy were inextricably connected under this conception and as a consequence the planning of economic life mirrored the planning of education (Ruiz, 2010)—a foundational idea of the curriculum field. According to Ruiz (2010) this connection between education and economy marginalizes other components of an educational theory aiming at democratic formation and access to non-instrumental forms of knowledge. One may also add that this instrumental understanding of education matches well with the technocratic concept of Curriculum Studies as *curriculum development* that became the predominant discourse within the Chilean educational reform. The arrival of Curriculum Studies was a rupture in Latin American educational history. Díaz Barriga and García-Garduño (2014) say:

> Before the 1960s, curriculum as a topic of educational concern was barely known in the region. Educational systems ran alongside a course of study that responded to diverse national traits. Educational thinking was circumscribed to topics related to the pedagogical and didactic, and in general, the characteristics of an efficiency-and-productivity based view of education were absent.
>
> (p. 11)[6]

Along with this turn to instrumental reason, the educational reforms begun in the 1960s meant also a rupture with previous reform movements that had had a more sociopolitical than an economic motif. It was also a rupture with regard to its main actor, since the previous reforms were mostly pushed by teacher movements. Now teachers were the targets of a reform developed by a group of experts whose developmentalist approach put educational planning at the core of the reform. In this context, the "new curricular conceptions of the North American Ralph Tyler and Benjamin Bloom" became a crucial element of the educational reform since they "emphasize curriculum planning" (Zemelman & Jara, 2006, p. 139). Mario Leyton was the main figure in the importation of these ideas into Chile. Leyton had been a student of Tyler's at the University of Chicago where he became a specialist in curriculum development. In Chile, Leyton joined the efforts of the educational reform. In fact, Leyton and Tyler coauthored *Planeamiento Educacional: Un Modelo Pedagógico* [Educational Planning: A Pedagogical Model] (1969), a book that may be fairly regarded as the foundational text of the field of curriculum in Chile. Leyton was the main educational theoretician of the reform (Ruiz, 2010; Zemelman & Jara, 2006); and he was convinced of the advantages that the criteria of flexibility and functionality contribute to the selection and organization of educational objectives and that "the development of behaviors gives to learning its power of shaping and its transference capacity" (Leyton, quoted in Zemelman & Jara, 2006, p. 143). To Leyton too, education and economic development are connected and the planning of education is crucial to the country's modernization. In a 1967 document published by the *Comisión de Planeamiento Integral de la Educación* [Integral Planning of Education Commission], he affirms that Chile is in a transitional stage from "a preindustrial society to another of an industrial type, which must be taken into consideration to define an educational structure that responds to the requirements of development" (Leyton, 1967, p. 60). Consequentially, science and technology were at the center of the reform's educational conception.

Not unconnected from the above, one of the main outcomes of Frei's reform was the creation of "a revitalized and technocratized educational infrastructure" (Fischer, 1979, p. 55). Above all, Fischer continues, "educational change emanated from a core of technicians or experts—at the CPEIP, the National Evaluation Service, the National Guidance Service and the like" (p. 55). The field of curriculum under what is now known as Tyler's rationale was imported along with that educational technology that offered to educational leaders a new language to trigger educational change, deploying an expert jargon. This was a mechanistic application of an intellectual device born in a different tradition. An actualization that seems too far away from the declared intention of Frei's, who, in his Message to the Chilean National Congress in May 1965, affirmed that as social thinkers "we have been until now the great imitators of history and of the theory of other peoples" (in Fischer, 1979, p. 41). Latin American dependence was not only economic but also intellectual and the deployment of developmentalist approaches in education during the 1960s shows how difficult it is to become a society that is not prevented from listening to its own voice.

In a broader sense, the 1970 election of Salvador Allende meant a failure of the not so subtle effort of the U.S. government strategy to support a "middle class revolution" that prevented *Latinoamérica* from following a path that could affect "American interests." Allende's *Via Chilena al Socialismo* [Chilean way to Socialism] provoked the consternation of imperial-minded U.S. policy makers. "We set the limits of diversity," Kissinger was heard to tell his staff as the United States initiated a series of covert operations against Allende (Kornbluh, 2003, p. xiii). This concern that the election of Allende caused in the U.S. government ended up in the 1973 military coup that ended Allende's government, interrupting the mythical constitutional democratic Chilean tradition. Repression was the first call of the inaugurated dictatorship that looked to fully silence any memory of the people standing up during the regressive 1960s. Fischer (1979) comments: "Within the first week, all the streets murals and political graffiti had been removed from the Mapocho River and from walls and fences all around Santiago. Similar actions were taken shortly thereafter in the provinces" (p. 127). What followed was torture, assassination, disappearance, and exile. Somehow, the violence of the repression resonates with another characteristic of the Chilean educational system, previous to the emphasis on the link between education and economy. That aspect of the educational system would come back strongly during the years to come when the silence would reign again: authoritarianism. The dictatorship may, thus, be read as the restoration of the culture of silence imposed by the European invasion that followed the mythic 1492.

The more the rise of the masses is emphasized in Latin America, the more the elite holding power, committed to foreign interests, will polarize against them. In this way, to the extent that the populist phase seems to indicate its goal by the intensification of popular pressures and an attempt to organize, the power elites, feeling ever more threatened, have no alternative but to end the process. By doing it repressively, denying the popular classes the right to express themselves and offering them a mythical education, they reactivate the old tradition of the "culture of silence" (Freire, 1970b, p. 47). Freire knew too well about the reactivation of the culture of silence that sent him into exile, given his struggle against it through his culture circles. In those circles the word of the *Otro* was heard breaking the culture of silence.

The Culture of Silence and Beyond

The expression "culture of silence" (1970a) was coined by Paulo Freire in his first writings. It is important to notice that this expression coming out from the margins of the periphery of the world-system is anything but provincial. Freire remarks that human beings belong in dialogue rather than in silence. "Human existence cannot be silent," (Freire, 1970b, p. 88), since "human life is life in conversation" (Maturana, 2008, p. 35). The world becomes human when named and to "exist, humanly, is to *name* the world, to change it" (Freire, 1970b, p. 88) with words that make it, once named, into a problem. That is why to Freire the silence of the culture of silence is hopeless. "Hopelessness is a form of silence" (Freire, 1970b, p. 91).

Grounded in this biographical and historical experience, Freire's[7] pedagogical-political project would be an answer to the Brazilian historical present and past. It would be to this issue that Freire will dedicate his doctoral dissertation[8] *Education and Present-Day in Brazil* which will be the basis for his *Educacion Como Practica de Libertad* (1965). The Brazil that Freire describes there is a country characterized by a secular authoritarianism and the silence in which its people has been kept. Freire's project stands up against that situation stating that "in alienated societies, men oscillate between ingenuous optimism and hopelessness" (Freire, 1973, p. 10). Therefore, "Our verbal culture corresponds to our inadequacy of dialogue, investigation, and research" (Freire, 1973, p. 33), he maintains. Freire perceives Brazil as a society in transition. Unfortunately, he laments, the Brazilian people are "unprepared to evaluate the transition critically" (Freire, 1973, p. 9). Moreover, Freire sees the capacity to talk and the capacity to self-determine connected. For him, without dialogue "self-government cannot exist: hence, self-government was almost unknown among us" (Freire, 1973, p. 21). The authoritarianism and the culture of silence are two sides of the same coin. In order to construct a democratic society in Brazil, Freire's educational praxis searches to break the culture of silence and authoritarianism. Freire is convinced that Brazilian people "could be helped to learn democracy through the exercise of democracy" (Freire, 1973, p. 32).

Freire arrived in Chile in 1964, continuing his exile that had begun in Bolivia some months before. He would stay in Chile for almost five years, until 1969, when he left for the United States and then for Geneva, where, working with the World Church Council, he will continue his work in Africa in the context of recently "decolonized" countries.[9] His Chilean exile coincided with Frei's government and his educational reform. It was during this period that Freire wrote his main works,[10] systematizing his educational-political practice in Brazil in the context of his work in Chile. In Chile, just as in Brazil, his work was focused on adult education and the education of the peasant, connected with the process of agrarian reform that the Chilean government was implementing.[11] Like the educational reform, the agrarian reform was part of the program forwarded by Alliance for Progress.[12] And both were thought of in the context of theories of economic development and modernization. Freire was familiar with programs, working under that approach in Brazil before his exodus.[13] However, it was in Chile that Freire made explicit his break with the developmentalist approach. Developmentalism becomes a fallacy when thinking historically. Dependence rather than underdevelopment explains Latin American misery. A developmentalist strategy remains trapped in the fallacy that blames *Latinoamérica* as guilty of its incapacity. The continent had been summoned into the world-system and become periphery, ergo dependent. The problem has then become resituated in a historical and planetary scale. Any effort of modernization in education or in agriculture would be a kind of cultural invasion if it relied on the *falacia desarrollista* [developmentalist fallacy] that in order to be you must become another who is not for himself but for someone else. Developmentalism asserts that by growth one becomes stage-appropriate, but in abstracting from particularity lived time is effaced in favor of linear progression in stages.

> The "delay" of peripheral capitalism is a "before" with respect to the "after" or "late" capitalism. What is not taking into account in this Eurocentric ideology, is that there is not such "before." Since 1992, the periphery is not a "before," but an "underneath": the exploited, the dominated, the origin of stolen wealth, accumulated in the dominating, exploiting "center." We repeat: the developmentalist fallacy thinks the "slave" is a "free lord" in his youthful stage, and like a child (Crude or barbarian).
>
> (Dussel, 1996, p. 5)

In such a cultural invasion "dialogue cannot exist. There is not such a thing as dialogical manipulation or conquest" (Freire, 1973, p. 104).

Domination and silence are inextricably connected, which is to say that the culture of silence is culture of domination.

The culture of silence is, according to him, characteristic of closed societies.[14] Those societies, in contrast to open societies, do not permit dialogue, which requires opening to the *Otro*. That is exactly the problem of the Brazilian transition to Freire: a closed society without democratic experience which must be the base for practicing democracy in an age that is coming along. That was for Freire the situation of all Latin American societies: societies where dialogue was denied to their peoples. "Herein lie the roots of Brazilian *mutism*" (Freire, 1973, p. 21), he wrote in his *Educación como Práctica de Libertad*, clarifying that silence did not mean "an absence of response, but rather a response that lacks a critical quality" (Freire, 1973, p. 21). This culture of silence was forged during "a colonial past of kings and viceroys; Crown representatives, oppression and reproof, of an elitist education not able to free men but able to forbid them the possibility of personal expression" (Freire, 1970b, p. 45).

Forged during the colonial times, the culture of silence survived during the postcolonial situation that for *Latinoamérica* started more than 200 years ago. Dussel has used this Freirian concept of culture of silence to describe the situation in which the oppressed have been kept silent by the enlightened elites and their Eurocentrism. This culture of silence has made the peoples of *Latinoamérica* "other than themselves" (Dussel, 1973, p. 152), strangers in their own land. While informing Latino American societies as a whole, both the dominating elites and the dominated peoples, Freire saw the rural areas of *Latinoamérica* as places where the culture of silence had endured more, obviously. Those areas were precisely where Freire worked the most.

The theme of silence shows itself dramatically in the work of the culture circles, suggesting a "structure of mutism in the face of the overwhelming force of the limit-situations[15]" (Freire, 1970b, p. 106). The cultural action through these culture circles looked to unfold the culture of silence as a "knowable object" to be critically addressed. "Through this liberating cultural action, inasmuch as it involves dialogue instead of cultural invasion, a cultural synthesis is accomplished" (Freire, 1970b, p. 49). In his Chilean experience working with peasants in areas that were part of the agrarian reform, Freire asked whether there was a possibility of dialogue while there is no change in the "structure that [was] the explanation of the silence of the peasants lies" (p. 109). He observed that "silence begins in one way or another to disappear in areas undergoing agrarian reform or subject to the indirect influence of such areas, as I observed in Chile" (p. 109). A dialogue that makes the causes of the silence into a problem would be, to Freire, the only way to break the silence of the peasant. An education that builds up a culture of freedom would come only out of surpassing the culture of silence. That would allow Latin American societies to become beings for themselves, to reach a new synthesis.

This intention was at the base of attempts by the thinkers of liberation to find the fundamental categories of the Latin American way of being in the world. This search for an authentic *pensamiento latinoamericano* [Latin American thinking] sought to overcome the uncritical transplant of foreign schools of thought. Therefore, the culture of silence is the negative point of departure that *Latinoamérica* must negate in order to affirm itself as such. In 1973, Dussel formulated this problematic in the following terms: "It is a restatement of Hegel's dialectics, its antecedents and possible surpasses, aiming for an adequate formulation of a concrete interpretive Latin American system" (p. 229). It is intriguing that Freire also begins his justification of the pedagogy of the oppressed with Hegel's dialectic of the master and the slave. Quoting Hegel, Freire analyzed the dialectics of relationship of the master and the oppressed in terms of their differences between their consciousnesses: "The one is independent, and its essential nature is to be for itself; the other is dependent, and its essence is life or existence for another. The former is the Master, or Lord, the latter the Bondsman" (quoted in Freire, 1970b, p. 49). In educational terms

> The teacher presents himself to his students as their necessary opposite; by considering their ignorance absolute, he-justifies his own existence. The students, alienated like the slave in the Hegelian dialectic, accept their ignorance as justifying the teachers existence—but, unlike the slave, they never discover that they educate the teacher.
> (Freire, 1970b, p. 72)

Just as for the slave or the student, for society to become a subject society, instead of a society that is an object of other ones, requires the raising of a consciousness that is not only in itself but it also able to "express itself or acquire self-awareness of it *for itself*" (Dussel, 2013, p. 315). Then the culture of silence becomes discourse, Dussel remarks. In the process of thinking its negativity from its praxis of liberation, *Latinoamérica* developed its educational contribution to the world: the pedagogy of liberation.

While interrupted by the U.S.-sponsored dictatorships that by the mid-1970s had taken over most Latin American countries, this political-pedagogical project also crossed the borders of *Latinoamérica* as a consequence of the exile of the intellectuals who survived the reinforcement of the culture of silence which followed Alliance for Progress.

The culture of silence "is predisposed to be "reactivated" in its manifestations under more favorable circumstances" (Freire, 1970b, p. 47), the Latin American pedagogue wrote from Harvard in 1970. Freire's *Pedagogy of the Oppressed* would be published almost simultaneously in *Latinoamérica* and the United States. This work,[16] of which Said called an "exilic imagination,"[17] became one of the main influences of the time. Perhaps, one of the most remarkable of those was the one upon the field of Curriculum Studies in the United States, which had also initiated its critique of the technological conception of curriculum. It may be fairly said that the 1970 publication of the *Pedagogy of the Oppressed* became an active force in a field that some years later would begin its own reconceptualization.[18] The 1973 Rochester Conference, the foundational moment of the reconceptualization, had Freire as the most referred author in the papers presented there by the keynote speakers, and a year later published under the title of *Heightened Consciousness, Cultural Revolution, and Curriculum Theory: The Proceedings of the Rochester Conference* (Pinar, 1974). Among those speakers was Maxine Greene, who began her presentation asserting that her "theme derive[s] in part from Paulo Freire, particularly from his notion that 'liberating education consists in acts of cognition'" (1974, p. 69). Maxine Greene had already referred extensively to Freire in her previous and better-known paper *Curriculum and Consciousness* (1971), a work that later would be included in Pinar's 1975 edited book, *Curriculum Theorizing: The Reconceptualists*. Pinar, who would become the main figure of the reconceptualization, had been also strongly influenced by Freire's work. In fact, Pinar's second paper, *Sanity, Madness, and the School* had as a subtitle *A Phenomenological Analysis of the Psychological Effects of 'Banking' Education* (1973). At this point, the affinity between the *Pedagógica Latinoamericana* and the reconceptualization of the field of curriculum is evident. Pinar wrote in 1976:

> From one perspective *currere* starts with Freire's Pedagogy of the Oppressed and with the major themes in that book. The first is that human vocation, ontologically, is humanization; the second is that to pedagogically act in accord with this meaning of the human endeavor is to dialogically encounter one's students; the third is to so encounter our students as to cultivate thought and action, a sort of praxis Freire terms "*Conscientização*."[19]
>
> (Pinar, 1976, p. 93)

Freire was compelling to a field which, according to Pinar (1974), in order to survive "must evolve morally and intellectually; it must evolve in consciousness" (p. ix). It was a field that had "forgotten what existence is" (1975, p. 396). What the moribund patient needed was *Conscientização*. This search would make the U.S. curriculum field to become a sort of "forum for exchange for, in Freire's "still useful" notion of "dialogical encounter" (Pinar, 1978, p. 65). The dialogical Latin American tradition preceded and somehow foresaw the later U.S. understanding of Curriculum Studies as complicated conversation. In a field aiming at internationalization, this southern concept of dialogical encounter become crucial, in a time when educational standardization threatened to reactivate at a global scale the culture of silence in which the Global South has been submerged since the beginning of modernity more than 500 years ago.

The Progressive 1990s and Appearance of the *Otro*

Although it was not a quiet warm morning, the group could still be outside to initiate the first meeting of the encounter we had organized under the title *Latinoamérica 500 Años y una Búsqueda* [Latinoamérica 500 years and a search]. We were two friends coming from the South, others from Santiago,[20] and some locals from Conception;[21] an older couple joined us. These were visiting Chile after almost 30 years. They had come to Chile in the 1960s as missionaries, we learned from introductory chatting. They had participated in workers' organizations and base communities,[22] mainly Catholic. Having fallen in love, they decided to abandon the habits, get married, and shortly after left for France, their home country. They told us they had followed with sadness the news from Chile during the years of dictatorship. They decided to come back and visit the country to see how things were changing in the transition to democracy underway in Chile since 1989. In that context our encounter had gotten their attention and they had asked to be invited.

Their story was not strange to me. My parents had met in a Catholic youth working-class organization,[23] so I had grown up listening to stories similar to theirs. What was surprising was their belief that most of their friends had been killed by the dictatorship, especially when they learned that my last name was Johnson and that I was the son of Pedro and Silvia, and that Julio was the son of Julio and Eliana, my godparents, some of the friends they had met almost three decades before. The couple insisted that they thought that the people they met must have been killed, given their political commitment. They also asked what the situation was since the transition to democracy had begun, and people seemed not to care about any political activity aiming at transformation; what had happened with all that movement? Another friend in the group answered: "Well, you can see that the kids of those people are here, in this encounter."

As a first activity, we explained why we had organized the encounter and emphasized why we had chosen the title of *Latinoamérica 500 Años y una Búsqueda*. The problem of *la identidad latinoamericana* [Latin American Identity] was self-evident for most of the attendees, so everyone seemed to agree that main word *búsqueda* was suitable to describe our self-reflection about being *latinoamericanos*. Pablo, a friend that had come from Angol in the *Region de la Araucanía*[24] [Araucanía Region], agreed that búsqueda was a good word to describe the Latin American existence, but he added: "however, that is your problem. We *Mapuche* people know who we are. We do not need to search for anything. We are *Mapuche—gente de la tierra* [people from the land]." He was right.

The *progressive* moment, perhaps the only one, is the emergence of the other as a legitimate other. The 1990s saw in *Latinoamérica* the emergence of the *Otro*, the *indio*. Rejecting the celebration of 500 years of the so-called discovery of *América* in 1992, they commemorated their *500 Años de resistencia* [500 years of resistance]. I lived that historical moment in relation with my study of Latin American history and liberation theology. Through that path I came to the field of education. At that time, Chile was going through the so-called transition to democracy, which at the second half of the decade embraced an educational reform. The educational reform was part of Frei's government, the son of the President that had implemented the educational reform in the regressive 1960s. In the United States it was the time when a reconceptualized field had already emerged: a field mapped in *Curriculum Understanding* (Pinar, Reynolds, Slattery, & Taubman, 1995). Those two decades, the 1970s and the 1980s reconceptualization in the United States were missed at that time in Chile, perhaps globally.

The Indio *as the* Otro

The *indio* is the denied part of the *mestiza* Latin American identity. As dual beings, Malinche's children, the *latinoamericanos* seem to be more inclined to their father's culture. This disposition makes us Eurocentric beings that deny our mother's culture. This is not unconnected from the historical trauma of the conquest. The *mestizo latinoamericano* reenacts the European cover-up of the *indio* as an *Otro* during the primal phenomenon of modernity. That cover up is already present in the word *indio* itself. For the European, the *indio* was "discovered" and became an identity that was brought into history from its Asian being, as O'Gorman pointed out in *The Invention of America* (1995). Dussel (2011) explains this in the following terms:

> The "appearance" of the Other, as a phantasm, the semi-naked indigenous, which Columbus saw on the beaches of the tropical islands of the western "Atlantic" "discovered" in October 1492, was rapidly covered by the mask of the "others," which the European imagined. They did not see the Indian: they imagined others already in their European memory. The Other was interpreted from the European "world"; it was an invention of Europe.
>
> (p. 191)

However, this is not the only possible point of view. Beyond the European and the Eurocentric understandings lies the voice of the *Otro*. To listen to that voice requires one to remain silent. This is the only possibility for conversation as intercultural dialogue. This was not the situation when the Latin American governments began to get ready for the celebration of the 500 years of the discovery of *América*. Nor was this the situation of Spain, which with this celebratory attitude wanted to show itself as a European country in its own continent. Nevertheless, the voices of the *indio* made themselves heard in spite of the culture of silence in which *Latinoamérica* had been re-submerged by the violence of the dictatorships following Alliance for Progress. After all, for the *pueblos originarios* [First Nations] of *América* that violence had been five centuries long.

In a continental encounter of *Native American* peoples held in Quito, Ecuador, in 1990, the "indios de América" [Indigenous people of America] (Declaración de Quito [Quito Declaration], 1990, p. 1) asserted that they had never "abandoned our [their] permanent struggle against the condition of oppression, discrimination and exploitation imposed on us [them] by the European invasion of our [their] ancestral territories" (p. 1). And they continued reaffirming their "deep rejection to the celebration of the Fifth Centenary. And the firm purpose of making that date into an occasion to strengthen our [their] unity and continental struggle toward our liberation" (p. 1). In this struggle, the document acknowledged the important role played by the "indigenous women" and the "need to widen woman's participation in our [their] organizations . . . as a key point in our [their but also our] political practice" (p. 1).

The *Quito Declaration* included also statements of special commissions, among them one that worked on education and religion. Through this work, the indigenous organizations present in the continental encounter defined education as "the exchange of wisdom and cultural values in a constant harmony between nature and humanity" (p. 7). Contrasting this understanding of education to the European education, the *Native Americans* affirmed that education "has only led us to a process of acculturation, submission and individualism, which carries the name of banking education" (p. 7). The text is rich in content and resonances.[25] Acculturation, as we have seen, is also the expression that Díaz-Barriga and García-Garduño (2014) use to describe the import of curriculum development in the 1970s. The document continues, saying that this European education, which is banking education, has devalued the "true millenary wisdom of the nations of *Abya-Yala*" (p. 7). This last term speaks of the equivocalness of the expression *América* (yes, also in *Latinoamérica*) when referring to the continent where native peoples lived before the invasion. Actually, there is not an equivalent to the standardizing term *América* by which these peoples' ancestral territories were named from Europe. *Abya-Yala* speaks of the need to take distance from that process and a wise attempt of naming things by their right name. *Abya-Yala* is a word spoken in the *Kuna* language meaning "mature land" and "land of vital blood." It is a composite word that comes from the word *abya*, meaning, blood and the word *yala*, meaning land or place. The expression *Abya-Yala* made its way through the continent as a part of the indigenous movement that took continental dimensions around the campaign for 500 years of resistance.

The *Mapuche* people also rejected the celebratory ambience of the Latin American governments previous to 1992. In their *Manifiesto de la Nación Mapuche con Relación a los 500 Años de Invasión y Colonización de Nuestro Continente* [Manifest of the *Mapuche* Nation in

Relation to the 500 Years of Invasion and Colonization of our Continent] the *Mapuche* people stated that they and other indigenous nations of the continent "continue existing in spite of the longest war of occupation we [they] had to face" (p. 1). And they affirm that "there was not such a discovery and full evangelization . . . but the invasion of our territory. This had as a consequence the largest genocide known in history, reaching more than 75 million of our brothers in our continent" (p. 2). That genocide was followed by the genocide "consisting in the negation of our existence" (p. 2). They also declared that there was no *Encuentro de dos Mundos* [Encounter of Two Worlds] since there was not the "coming closer of two human communities but the imposition of one over the other" (p. 3). After clarifying their diagnosis, the *Mapuche* people demanded from the Chilean nation state and the Catholic Church

> to allow us [them] the planning and implementation of an educational system of our own that procures the rescue and development of our cultural values for the affirmation of our identity. . . . the end of an evangelization and pastoral of alliance with the dominating system, genocide of indigenous, to permit a practice of authentic pastoral of companionship, dialogue and respect toward our struggles as one of the statements arising within the liberatory church.
>
> (pp. 4–5)

Interestingly, as a continental organization, the *Mapuche* traditional organization included explicitly in their declaration of the 500 years of resistance elements that resonate with the Latin American thinking of liberation born by the end of the 1960s, and specifically of liberation theology. This was the tradition within which Freire forged his thought as the main figure of the *Pedagógica Latinoamericana*. It is certainly a tradition that had heard the completely *Otro*. In that regard, this Latin American tradition sought its precedents in the critique of the conquest, which "may be considered the first, implicit, Liberation Philosophy" (Dussel, 1996, p. 2). In the 1990s, and around the commemoration of the mythic 1492, the now much more mature thinking of liberation addressed more deeply the decolonizing turn that began at the end of the regressive 1960s.

> Because the originary experience of liberation philosophy consists in discovering the massive "fact" of domination, of the constitution of a subjectivity as "lord" of another subjectivity at the world level (From the beginning of the European expansion in 1492, the originary event of "modernity") . . . This originary "experience"—lived by all Latin Americans . . . is best indicated by the category of "Autrui" (Another person as Other), as *pauper*.
>
> (Dussel, 1996, p. 80)

It is now the turn for the thinking of this *Latinoamérica mestiza* to discover the *Otro* covered up inside itself also. This is at the center of the Latin American thinking of liberation and its educational tradition.

The Pensamiento Latinoamericano *and the Question of the* Otro

Born in the underside of modernity, the *pensamiento latinoamericano* understood very well that the *Otro* is the other face of modernity. Dussel wrote in his dialogue with the main European and North American philosophers, such as Karl Otto Apel, Paul Ricoeur, Richard Rorty, and Charles Taylor, regarding the status of his Latin American thinking:

> Latin America is neither pre-, anti-, nor post-modern; and, for that reason, we cannot "realize" fully an incomplete modernity (as Jürgen Habermas suggests optimistically), because as the slave (before the "Lord" of slavery) we have "paid" with our misery, with our "non-Being" (since 1492 as colonial world, first, and since 1810 as neocolonial world); for the "Being," the primitive accumulation and successive supersessions of the "happy" capitalism of the center, and even of those who are so-called delayed.
>
> (Dussel, 1996, pp. 3–4)

The great Latin American philosopher is drawing here on dependency theory—a Latin American approach developed both alongside and in opposition to the theories of modernization and development under which the problem of *Latinoamérica* has been defined by international organizations since the 1950s. The move from developmentalism to dependency theory was part of the intellectual biography of many Latin American thinkers in the 1960s, and also of others. One remarkable case is that of Gunder Frank (1973, 1979), a former student of Milton Friedman who came to Chile, and through whose scholarship dependency theory was subsumed into Wallerstein's (2004) world-system theory. The year 1492 inaugurated the beginning of a system at a global scale that situated Europe as a center of the world that expanded itself in its making the rest of the world into its peripheries. This concept of world-system shed light on the Eurocentric confusion that understands "the evolution of subjectivity within the limits of Europe not only with universality . . . but also with globality" (Dussel, 2011, p. 216). Modernity is the management of Europe's new situation made possible by the invasion of *América*. This Eurocentrism underlines conceptually and historically the modern phenomena of racism and ethnocentrism. Indeed, Dussel (1996) elaborates, modernity

> inaugurates the first irrationalism in a global scale: racism and ethnocentrism as expressions of the superiority of Europe over the other

races and peripheral cultures (eurocentrism), *ad extra*, with two holocausts: the holocaust of the conquest of America with more than 15 million exterminated Indians; and the holocaust of slavery with 13 million Africans (more than 30 percent would die in the Middle Passage—the transatlantic transport). The second irrationalism is Nazism as the corollary *ad intra* of racist eurocentrism; the superiority of the supposed Aryan race over the Jewish race, with the third modern holocaust of the systematic assassination of 6 million Jews.

(p. 50)

Taking the underside of modernity, which is the Latin American exteriority[26] but also the Global South's, as *locus enunciationis*, Levinas's *Autre* [Other] is not only the Jew but also the *indio* and the *negro*. They are the exteriority (*ad intra* and *at extra*) of Europe, the majority of today's humanity, the Global South. This notion of exteriority is the great contribution of Levinas to the thinking of liberation. Levinas's student writes:

> Alterity moves from complete Exteriority, prior to the process of slavery, to an oppressive subsuming in America, which negates all recognition of the dignity of the Other, through an unheard-of inhuman bloody violence, the origin of the process of Modernity as the hidden face of exteriority of the system, unknown also by modern and contemporary philosophy. American colonization and African slavery have left indelible marks and demand a deep practical and theoretical, ethical, cultural and economic-political transformation of the alterity excluded for centuries.
>
> (Dussel, 2011, p. 183)

These *Otro* were thought about as immature, barbarian, child-like, not-fully human beings. "At best, the Spaniards considered the Indians coarse, childlike, immature (*Unmunding*), needing patient evangelization" (Dussel, 1995, p. 54).

This needy child-like being is the foundation of the developmentalist fallacy that thinks "the "slave" is a "free lord" in its youthful stage, ("crude or barbarian"). It does not understand that the slave is the dialectical "other face" of domination: the as-always, the "other part of the exploitative relation" (Dussel, 1995, p. 57). It is not a problem of evolutionary development but of the power positions in a world-system. There is no "before" for the delay of peripheral countries "with respect to the 'after' or 'late' capitalism . . ., the periphery is not a 'before,' but an 'underneath': the exploited, the dominated, and the origin of stolen wealth, accumulated in the dominating, exploiting 'center'" (Dussel, 1996, p. 5). This Eurocentric approach remained alive after the Latin American emancipation, being reenacted by *mestizo* republics that rejected the *indio* inside them. This is the living contradiction of the *mestizo latinoamericano*, that syncretic-hybrid being brought into life along this process. "*Mestizos* live in their own flesh the contradictory tension of modernity as both emancipation and sacrificial myth" (p. 55), Dussel (1995) insists in his Frankfurt lectures.[27] It cannot be otherwise since the birth of *mestizo* is a consequence of the primal phenomenon of modernity, a historical rape. The erotic encounter between bodies of different cultures existed but they were the exception; what predominated was erotic violence over the indigenous women by the European men. The conquest of *Abya-Yala* was also an erotic conquest. The dramatic violent connection between Europe and this Mature Land, *Abya-Yala*, is through the female *india* body. The result is evident in the body of the *mestizo latinoamericano*. However, this is not the only way in which the *mujer india* [Indian woman] became a link between the two worlds.

I have already said that conversation as intercultural dialogue became impossible from the very beginning of modernity. Todorov in his *The Conquest of America: The Question of the Other* (1984) points out the material limits of not just such a conversation but of mere communication. As evident as that may be, it is important to remember that there was a linguistic gap at least during the first decades of the conquest, which progressed from its Caribbean centers to the rest of *América*. This communicative gap was overcome by improvised translators. *La Malinche* was not just a *mujer india* given to Cortez as a sexual gift: she was also Cortez's translator since she learned Spanish[28] and spoke also her mother tongue and other indigenous languages. Most of the codex of the first decades of the conquest picture the Malinche, then *Dona Marina* [Mrs. Marina], speaking next to Cortez.

> La Malinche, the indian woman who became an interpreter, guide, mistress, and confidante of Cortes during the times of the conquest. Although her voice has been silenced, her presence and functions are documented in the chronical. For that reason she may be considered the first women of Mexican literature, just as she is considered the first mother of the Mexican nation and the Mexican eve, symbol of national betrayal.
>
> (Messinger, 1991. p. 2)

La Malinche, to which the image of the *mestizo latinoamericano* is almost automatically deferred, is already a *mestizo* in her indigenous pre-invasion world, since she had been given away by her father. She learned the language of her new male owner while not forgetting her mother tongue. *La Malinche* situates the idea of conversation at the center of human intercourse. The body of the *mujer india* speaks, to the attentive listener, of what is at stake in any encounter where the humanity of the *Otro* is not fully guaranteed. Therefore "the illocutionary component, the practical-communicative relationship itself with the Other in face-to-face proximity, cannot be reduced to a communicative-linguistic act. The *linguistic*, like the *erotic* or the *economic* aspects of the practical relation, is a moment of the relationship" (Dussel, 1996, p. 32). The inclusion of the *Otro* within the European totality is made by excluding him-her from the community of communication, with its economic, erotic, and pedagogical intertwining. During the conquest, in no place is this clearer than in the *india* woman's body. Her cry while being raped is a word that becomes an interpellation for those that want to hear. For certain philosophies of language, Freire criticizes, this is ignored, through their "word juggling, which reduces to silence the cry of the oppressed" (Freire, 1970a, p. 177). This is the originary interpellation of the *Otro* of Europe, the originary interpellation to the modern project, which cannot interpret "the pain of the oppressed" (Freire, 1970a, p. 177). That is why the counter discourse to modernity has the critique of the conquest as its first expression. This critique announced the search of the Latin American thinkers of liberation.

> In 1514, three years before the beginning of the Lutheran Reformation, when Maquiavelli was writing The Prince, following Antón de Montecinos and Pedro de Córdova, Bartolomé [de las Casas] changed the existential project and was transformed from "encomienda priest" into "defender of the indians." Immediately he discovered in the Other, as Horkheimer would say, the misery in which the conquest has reduced the indian to an "original negativity."
> (Dussel, 2011, p. 198)

The culture of silence that Freire criticized is an imposition and also consequence of this historical trauma. It was also pushed forward by the cultural monologue of the Eurocentric project that had underlined education in *Latinoamérica* since that primal event. Negating that culture of silence, a negation of a negation, the *Pedagógica Latinoamericana* emerges as a pedagogy of listening. The listening that acknowledges the *Otro* as an *Otro* and celebrates his word is the affirmative moment of this Latin American pedagogy. The attentive listener is able to understand even that a cry, that is not yet a word, speaks.

A Pedagogy of Listening

> The expressive revelation of the people, which is welcomed only in silence, is the beginning of semiotic liberation. Its dynamism is the mobilization of the people itself, in whose exposition the provocative word is liberated.
> (Freire, 1970a, p. 125)

Freire's pedagogy begins by silence. Not the silence of the culture of silence brought into being to keep the peoples of *Latinoamérica* in silence, but the silence that makes dialogue possible. Hence the oppressed or the students are not just passive listeners, or listening objects, to use Freire's language. When the teacher is only the narrating subject, the students not only remain in the culture of silence, which is the most relevant consequence, but also the contents of the education "in the process of being narrated become lifeless and petrified" (Freire, 1970a, p. 71). Even more, beginning with silence the very contents of education are defined in dialogue. Educationally speaking, this dialogue is always intergenerational as well as intercultural. Better, intercultural and intergenerational dialogue presupposes each other. Consequentially, the attentiveness to the *Otro* that silence allows makes education into co-education.

Putting silence at the center of dialogical education, which is education for liberation, we are educated by the word of the *Otro*. Through her word the *Otro* reveals itself to us. Dialogue cannot occur "between those who want to name the world and those who do not wish this naming" (Freire, 2000, p. 88). Only in silence can we can listen to the *Otro* naming her world.

Freire speaks beautifully of this in his *Pedagogy of Hope* (1994). Let's listen:

> The speaker speaks in a hollow, silenced space and not in a space that is the presence of listening. Conversely, the space of the democratic-minded teacher who learns to speak by listening is interrupted by the intermittent silence of his or her own capacity to listen, waiting for that voice that may desire to speak from the depths of its own silent listening. The importance of silence in the context of communication is fundamental.[29]
>
> (p. 84)

The pedagogy of the oppressed begins with a pedagogy of listening. This pedagogy of listening is methodologically devised in what Freire (1970a) calls "thematic investigation" that aims to listen to the *Otro*'s naming of the world. This is to say, in Freire's words, "people's thematic universe," which is what thematic investigation seeks to discover. This listening takes place through the concrete listening to the "tapes recorded during the decoding sessions and studying the notes taken" (Freire, 1970a, p. 119). The "generative themes" coded in images come out of this listening to the people's thematic universe, inaugurating "the dialogue of education as the practice of freedom" (Freire, 1970a, p. 96). This is the educational practice within the culture circles as opposed to the pedagogical practice taking place in schools.

The attentive listener to the *Pedagógica Latinoamericana* is also the attentive listener of Levinas. We read in *La Liberación Latinoamericana y Emmanuel Levinas* (Dussel & Guillot, 1975) [The Latin American Liberation and Emanuel Levinas] that the "exteriority of every system points to the insufficiency of ontology and the need for a more radical understanding requires listening to the voice of the alterity, which leads outside of the self-reflexive thinking of the Same" (p. 80). The other's voice as a trans-ontological word, heard by the attentive listener, breaks the culture of silence in "respect for someone, for the freedom of the other" (Dussel, 1985, p. 59). This *Otro* appears as such only when we see the *indio*, the woman and the child as fully human—as the exteriority of the European-male-adult man.

Drawing on this Levinasian notion of exteriority the *Pedagógica Latinoamericana*, as a part of the philosophy of liberation, acknowledges the child as "distinct, not merely different, from the couple; the child is the other from whom one always has to learn how to listen in silence to the new revelation that is brought to past history as tradition" (Dussel, 1985, p. 89). For this pedagogy of liberation, in "the origin of words there is the other, who "speaks" by presence" (p. 117) and before whom "a silent responsibility" (p. 118) must be kept, waiting for his/her revelation. This attitude requires the cultivation of an ethical consciousness which is helped by the cultivation of silence.

Leaving the Regressive-Progressive *Kraftfeld*

By the end of the 1990s, my body had reached adulthood after roaming an uneven border space located among disciplines of theology-philosophy, history, and education. Those wandering years did not prevent me from cultivating in liminal terrains; I was nourished by memories of those landscapes in the healthy existence of a nomadic life. I have always enjoyed walking landscapes that resist complete cultivation. And yet, along the years, some of those places became familiar; they transformed into something similar to a home. I have cultivated there, but not without reluctance. Nevertheless, in my intellectual garden there has always been room for wild herbs to grow. I like to think this is part of being a "Franciscan," which has always been part of my life. I like to think too that is part of the *Mapuche* that is also part of my *mestizo* body. My father was a Capuchin novice before he left *Padre Las Casas*, a town located in the center of the *Mapuche* territory, on a path that would eventually take him first to *Chillán*[30] then *Concepcion*; where he met my mother. She had come there from *Cabrero* with my Grandma and my Aunt Lucy. It was, also, in a Franciscan church where as a child, promising not to get bored, I accompanied my Auntie Lucy and my Grandma to mass after listening to *México Canta* [Mexico sings] and *Con Permiso Soy el Tango* [Excuse me, I am *Tango*], on Radio *Almirante Latorre*. It was at that same church, I learned later, that my parents met and participated in the *Acción Católica* [Catholic Action] during the regressive 1960s; the same church in which at the beginning of the progressive 1990s I learned the Franciscan way of life and read for first time the works of Fray Leonardo Boff. *Francisco de*

Asís: Ternura y Vigor (1985) [Francis from Asis: Tenderness and Vigor] was a reading that led me to my study of theology on finishing high school, where I had come after leaving a vocational school, not fully aware of what I was doing.

> I never thought of going to college. Vocational school was the goal. I needed to have something soon. Nevertheless, I got into college. I spent three years studying law; in the third year I attended less and less. I read more social science books and liberation theology than my law books. My life was church, politics, and university. They were almost the same; they were learning and political spaces. I decided to study history. I thought that it would help me understand the world, transform it. I felt very ignorant at that time, I still do. That was why I studied history. It was at the end that I realized how important education was for me and how education could change people's lives. I realized that education had always been part of my life. Education was the new space to create a better world.
> (Johnson-Mardones, 2014, p. 251)

At the end of my years studying history, education came into my life. The bridge was the teaching of history, what we call *Didactica de la Historia* [Didactic of History]. That became the main focus of my study. *Latinoamérica* remained important, but my thesis would not be on Latin American popular religiosity but on a history of Concepción and a methodological approach to its teaching. It was neither in history nor in education but in an area in which the two converged. It was not an individual but a collective work. At that time, I realized that working with young people and education had always been part of my life. Maybe, at that moment of my life, my education had changed me. Education changed my life. That conviction was already part of my personal mythology.[31]

Notes

1. For more information, see Bellei, Cabalin, & Orellana (2014); Bellei & Cabalin (2013).
2. The Spanish term *vivir* as different from existir is explained in a footnote as follows: "In the English language, the terms "live" and "exist" have assumed implications opposite to their etymological origins. As used here, "live" is the more basic term, implying only survival; "exist" implies a deeper involvement in the process of "becoming" (Freire, 1970a, p. 98).
3. The *Tlatelolco* Massacre took place in October 2, 1968 in the Plaza de la Tres Culturas [Square of Three Cultures] in Tlatelolco Mexico City, Mexico. Student demonstrations in the Plaza de las Tres Culturas were bloodily repressed by the government, having as a result the death of more than 300 students.
4. Priista refers to PRI, Partido Revolucionario Institucional [Institutional Revolutionary Party]. Literally, this means a member or related to this party.

5. Free translation.
6. Free translation.
7. Paulo Reglus Neves Freire was born on Recife in 1921 being the youngest of four children of a middle-class family. Paulo's family left Recife for Jaboatao in 1932. That moving day, they also leave its "social place," as middle-class people, affected by the great depression—a world economic crisis whose effects reached Freire's family as it reached many other families, globally. "We left Recife due to the difficulties our family had begun to experience two or three years earlier; one of my maternal uncles Rodavalho, was forced to propose the move. The difficulties would have been felt earlier if it had not been for my uncle's help when my father became inactive due to his health," (Freire, 1996, p. 27) he recalls. Therefore, he continues "born into a middle-class family that suffered the impact of the economic crisis of 1929, we became connective kids. We participated in the world of those who are well, even though we had very little to eat ourselves, and in the world of kids from very poor neighborhoods on the outskirts of town (Freire, 1996, p. 21).
8. Based on his experience at SESI, "Freire defended his doctoral dissertation at the University of Recife and was appointed professor of the history and philosophy of education at the University of Pernambuco. The thesis, entitled Educação e atualidade brasileira [Education and Present-Day Brazil] dealt with silence and resistance in postcolonial Brazilian education" (Schugurensky, 2011, p. 19).
9. It is in *Pedagogy in process: The letters to Guinea-Bissau* (1978), where Freire reports about that experience.
10. It would be in his exile in Chile where the formulation of Freire's proposal will get written in his worldwide recognized *Pedagogy of the Oppressed* (1970a). In that regard, Freire affirms that it was "in the intense experience I was having in Chilean society—my own experience of their experience, which always sent me back in my mind to my Brazilian experience, whose vivid memory I had brought with me into exile—that I wrote *Pedagogy of the Oppressed*, in 1967 and 1968" (Freire, 1994, p. 52). The learning process that had taken place in political-pedagogical practice in Brazil was "consolidating in [my] Chilean practice and in the theoretical reflection I made upon that practice" (Freire, 1994, p. 43). Freire's discourses representing for his main works has Chile as a context of formulation. This context does not just tell us about his writing as writing in exile but also as writing from the borders. Those borders are the borders of the educational system represented by Freire's work in agrarian reform and adult education while the mainstream of schooling in Chile is going through an educational reform informed by educational planning.
11. Introducing his most important work, *Pedagogy of the Oppressed*, Freire asserts that his pedagogical-political proposal results from his "observations during six years of political exile, observations which have enriched those previously afforded by my [his] educational activities in Brazil" (Freire, 1970a, p. 35). Those Brazilian activities refer to his professional practice in three main spaces: Social Service of Industry (SESI), the Movement for Popular Culture, and the University of Pernambuco. It was in 1947 when Freire joined Social Service of Industry (SESI) in the Regional Department of Pernambuco; "where I . . . was involved in the most important political-pedagogical practice of my life," (p. 81). In this period of his life, Freire gets familiar with the perspective of national development and the role that education must fulfill (Pereira, 1980).
12. Commenting on the Brazilian context, Schugurensky (2011) affirms that "partly in response to the increasing unrest arising throughout Latin America

and with the background of the Cold War, in 1961 the United States created the Alliance for Progress to promote economic cooperation between North and South America, with the goal of increasing economic growth and reducing poverty. The Alliance for Progress established a U.S. Agency for International Development (AID) office for Brazil in Recife, considered a security threat due to the expansion of the Peasant Leagues" (p. 20).
13. To Pereira (1980), for example, Freire's educational thought must be understood in the ideological context of the 1950s and its *nacionalismo-desenvolvista* [developmentalist nationalism]. Schugurensky (2011) asserts that throughout "the 1950s and early 1960s, Brazilian political, social, and intellectual life was burgeoning" and that it "was a historical moment characterized by the emergence of developmentalism, an independent model of national development that took into account the needs of the poor" (p. 19). Therefore, it seems fair to claim that this discussion was the main intellectual context of Freire's writings before 1965.
14. Freire (1973) refers here to Karl Popper's work *The Open Society and its Enemies* (1966).
15. The concept of limit situation is found in Jaspers, that part of existentialism that in Germany did not fall into fascism, according to Sartre. Freire takes the concept from Viera Pinto. Freire (1970b) writes: "Professor Alvaro Vieira Pinto analyzes with clarity the problem of "limit-situations, using the concept without the pessimistic aspect originally found in Jaspers. For Vieira Pinto, the "limit-situations" are not "the impassable boundaries where possibilities end, but the real boundaries where all possibilities begin**; they are not "the frontier which separates being from nothingness, but the frontier which separates being from nothingness but the frontier which separates being from being more" Alvaro Vieira Pinto, *Consciencia e Realidade Nacional* (Rio de Janeiro, 1960), Vol. II, p. 284" (p. 99)
16. In his *The Pedagogy of Hope: Reliving Pedagogy of the Oppressed* (1994), Freire will say that the four-and-one-half years he lived in Chile "were years of a profound learning process" (Freire, 1994, p. 41). It was the first time, he continues, "that I had the experience of distancing myself geographically, with its epistemological consequences from Brazil" (Freire, 1994, p. 41). That geographical distance is now complemented by the temporal distance of almost two and a half decades passed since the publication of the *Pedagogy of the Oppressed* (1970a), a book "appeared at in an intensively troubled moment in History" (Freire, 1994, p. 120)—the time that he lived in his Chilean exile radicalized Freire.
17. McCarthy (2006) has called our attention to the issues of movement related to the development of one's intellectual project. Writing in the context of the black-Caribbean diaspora, also part of the tradition of the oppressed, McCarthy relates the "diasporic intellectual formation" that "brings into sharp view the remorseless process of cultural porosity and the consequential attrition of the nexus between black identities and fixed geographies of place" (p. 61). That diasporic intellectual formation—that exilic imagination, as Said would say—enables a differential consciousness that can be considered part of the tradition of the oppressed. This obviously includes what we may call a colonial differential consciousness.
18. I worked on this topic based on a close reading of the first works of the reconceptualization (Johnson-Mardones, 2015). In that text I presented "an in-progress interpretation of Curriculum Studies as an international conversation. I went back to the seminal texts of the reconceptualization of the field of Curriculum Studies in the United States in the 1970s, hoping that a close reading of them would provide some connections between the main authors

of that movement and the work of Paulo Freire. My intention is to show that these writers engaged in intellectual conversation with Freire's work at the time, although the field may now have forgotten how important this influence was for those early involved in reconceptualizing curriculum. Freire's concept such as *conscientização*, humanizing education, liberating education are important concepts in which these scholars elaborate to talk back to the mainstream of the field conceived exclusively as curriculum development. Freire's work was also a taking back to that rationale that had arrived in Latin America in the 1960s as a new educational technology. Freire's *Pedagogy of the Oppressed* appeared strongly influencing to the U.S. reconceptualization of the field in the 1970s. The reconceptualized field of curriculum was also international from the very first moment" (p. 1).

19. The word *Conscientização*, usually attributed to Freire was developed for a Brazilian team working at SESI. Freire also affirmed that it was Mons. Helder Camara that insisted he use it.
20. Santiago is the capital of Chile.
21. Concepción is the second largest city in Chile and is located 500 kilometers south from Santiago.
22. Comunidades Eclesiales de Base (CBS) [Base Church Communities] are grassroots Catholic communities.
23. The Ación Católica [Catholic Action] had many divisions according to the occupation of their members. My parents met in the Juventud Obrera Católica (JOC) [Working Class Catholic Youth].
24. The *Región de la Araucanía* is located in the South of Chile, approximately 800 kilometers south of Santiago and it is historically the territory of *Mapuche* people.
25. A gracious submission to the U.S. predominance in the region, which resonates with Pinar's (2012) parallel of the submission that teachers are asked to perform and the submission that married women are asked to comply with in conservative religious conceptions of marriage; and the Freirean term of banking education seems to be heard across cultures.
26. Levinas (2004) affirms that exteriority "taken as the presence of being signifies the resistance of the social multiplicity to the logic that totalizes the multiple" (p. 292).
27. The Frankfurt lectures correspond to a series of lectures given by Dussel at the University of Frankfurt in 1991 with the occasion of the upcoming 1992 commemoration. The texts comprising those lectures were published as *The invention of the Americas: Eclipse of "the other" and the myth of modernity* (1995).
28. "Malintzin comes to be known as la lengua, literally meaning the tongue. La lengua was the metaphor used, by Cortés and the chroniclers of the conquest, to refer to Malintzin the translator. However, she not only translated for Cortés and his men, she also bore his children. Thus, a combination of Malintzin-translator and Malintzin-procreator becomes the main feature of her subsequently ascribed treacherous nature" (Alarcón, 2003, p. 34).
29. On the one hand, Freire (1994) continues, "it affords me space while listening to the verbal communication of another person and allows me to enter into the internal rhythm of the speaker's thought and experience that rhythm as language. On the other hand, silence makes it possible for the speaker who is really committed to the experience of communication rather than to the simple transmission of information to hear the question, the doubt, the creativity of the person who is listening" (p. 84).
30. Chillán is a city about an hour driving from Concepción, close to the Andes Mountains.

31. Regarding a *mystory* as unit of interpretation in interpretive ethnography, Denzin (1997) has asserted that "mystory is simultaneously a personal mythology, a public story, and a performance that critiques." Therefore, the approach by using the expression "personal mythology" acknowledges what Bourdieu calls the "biographical illusion," and it denies what Derrida does as "metaphisys of present" in writing lives. "The autobiographical story stands somewhere between personal myths and personal fictions. . . . We reread our own story to find the mythic-fictive threads that we have woven through them" (Grumet, 2015, p. 175).

References

Alarcón, N. (2003). Traddutora, Traditora: A paradigmatic figure of Chicana feminism. In M. C. Gutmann, F. V. Matos Rodríguez, L. Stephen, & P. Zavella (Eds.). *Perspectives on Las Americas: A reader in culture, history and representation* (pp. 33–49). Maldem, MA: Blackwell Publishers.

Bellei, C., & Cabalin, C. (2013). Chilean student movements: Sustained struggle to transform a market-oriented educational system. *Current Issues in Comparative Education*, 15(2), 108–123.

Bellei, C., Cabalin, C., & Orellana, V. (2014). The 2011 Chilean student movement against neoliberal educational policies. *Studies in Higher Education*, 39(3), 426–440.

Benjamin, W. (2008). *The work of art in the age of its technological reproducibility, and other writings on media*. Cambridge, MA: Belknap Press of Harvard University Press.

Benjamin, W. (2004). Goethe's elective affinities. In M. P. Bullock & M. W. Jennings (Eds.) (1996–2002). *Walter Benjamin: Selected writings, Volume 1 1913–1926* (pp. 297–360). Cambridge, MS: Harvard University Press.

Benjamin, W. (1999). *The arcades project*. Cambridge, MA: Belknap Press of Harvard University Press.

Benjamin, W. (1968). *Illuminations*. New York, NY: Schocken Books.

Boff, L. (1985). *San Francisco de Asís, ternura y vigor*. Barcelona: San Terrae.

De Alba, A. (2011). Footprints and marks on the intellectual history of curriculum studies in Mexico. In W. F. Pinar (Ed.) (2011a). *Curriculum studies in Mexico: Intellectual histories, present circumstances* (pp. 49–74). New York, NY: Palgrave Macmillan.

Declaración de Quito [Quito Declaration]. (1990, July 21). *Primer Encuentro Continental de Pueblos Indígenas*.

Denzin, N. K. (2013a). Interpretive autoethnography. In S. L. Holman Jones & C. Ellis (Eds.). *Handbook of autoethnography* (pp. 123–142). New York, NY: Left Coast Press.

Denzin, N. K. (2013b). *Interpretive autoethnography*. Thousand Oaks, CA: Sage Publications.

Denzin, N. K. (1997). Performance texts. In W. G. Tierney & Y. S. Lincoln (Eds.). *Representation and the text: Re-framing the narrative voice*. Albany, NY: State University of New York Press.

Denzin, N. K. (1989). *Interpretive biography*. Newbury Park, CA: Sage Publications.

Díaz-Barriga, A., & García-Garduño, J. M. (2014). *Desarrollo del curriculum en América Latina: Experiencia de diez países*. Buenos Aires: Miño y Dávila editores.

Diaz-Barriga, F. (2011). Curriculum studies in Mexico: Current circumstances. In W. F. Pinar (Ed.). *Curriculum studies in Mexico: Intellectual histories, present circumstances* (pp. 91–110). New York, NY: Palgrave Macmillan.

Dussel, E. (2013). *Ethics of liberation in the age of globalization and exclusion.* Durham: Duke University Press.

Dussel, E. (2011). *Politics of liberation: A critical world history.* London: SCM Press.

Dussel, E. (1996). *The underside of modernity: Apel, Ricoeur, Rorty, Taylor, and the philosophy of liberation.* Atlantic Highlands, NY: Humanities Press.

Dussel, E. (1995). *The invention of the Americas: Eclipse of "the other" and the myth of modernity.* New York, NY: Continuum.

Dussel, E. (1985). *Philosophy of liberation.* New York, NY: Orbis Books.

Dussel, E. (1973). *Para una ética de la liberación latinoamericana.* Buenos Aires: Siglo Veintiuno Argentina Editores. V1.

Dussel, E., & Guillot, D. (1975). *Liberación latinoamericana y Emmanuel Levinas.* Buenos Aires: Editorial Bonum.

Fanon, F. (2004). *The wretched of the earth.* New York, NY: Grove Press.

Fanon, F. (1967). *Black skin, white masks.* New York, NY: Grove Press.

Fischer, K. B. (1979). *Political ideology and educational reform in Chile, 1964–1976.* Los Angeles, CA: UCLA Latin American Center Publications.

Frank, A. G. (1979). *Dependent accumulation and underdevelopment.* New York, NY: Monthly Review Press.

Frank, A. G. (1973). *Capitalismo y subdesarrollo en América Latina.* Buenos Aires: Siglo Veintiuno.

Freire, P. (1996). *Letters to Cristina: Reflections on my life and work.* New York, NY: Routledge.

Freire, P. (1994). *Pedagogy of hope: Reliving pedagogy of the oppressed.* New York, NY: Continuum.

Freire, P. (1978). *Pedagogy in process: The letters to Guinea-Bissau.* New York, NY: Seabury Press.

Freire, P. (1973). *Education for critical consciousness.* New York, NY: Seabury Press.

Freire, P. (1970a/2000). *Pedagogy of the oppressed.* New York, NY: Continuum.

Freire, P. (1970b). *Cultural action for freedom.* Cambridge, MA: Harvard Educational Review.

Freire, P. (1965). *La educación como práctica de la libertad.* Santiago de Chile: ICIRA.

Glazman, R. (2011). Revisiting curriculum studies. En W. F. Pinar (Ed.). *Curriculum studies in Mexico: Intellectual histories, present circumstances* (pp. 165–180). New York, NY: Palgrave Macmillan.

Greene, M. (1974). Curriculum, consciousness and cognition. In W. F. Pinar (Ed.). *Heightened consciousness, cultural revolution, and curriculum theory: The proceedings of the Rochester conference* (pp. 69–84). Berkeley, CA: McCutchan Pub. Corp.

Greene, M. (1971). Curriculum and consciousness. In W. F. Pinar (Ed.) (1975/2000). *Curriculum theorizing: The reconceptualization* (pp. 299–320). Troy, NY: Educator's International Press.

Grumet, M. (2015). In W. F. Pinar & M. R. Grumet. *Toward a poor curriculum.* Kingston, NY: Educator's International Press.

Jay, M. (1993). *Force fields: Between intellectual history and cultural critique.* New York, NY: Routledge.
Johnson-Mardones, D. (2015). Freire and the U.S. reconceptualization: Remembering curriculum as international conversation. *Transnational Curriculum Inquiry, 12*(1), 3–12.
Johnson-Mardones, D. (2014). Crying a thesis. *Qualitative Inquiry, 20*(3), 248–252.
Kornbluh, P. (2003). *The Pinochet file: A declassified dossier on atrocity and accountability.* New York, NY: New Press.
Levinas, E. (2004). *Totality and infinity: An essay on interiority.* Pittsburg, PN: Duquesne University Press.
Leyton, M. (1967). *Documento de trabajo.* Santiago, Chile: Comisión de Palneamiento Integral de la Educación.
Leyton, M., & Tyler, R. (1969). *Planeamiento educacional: Principios básicos del curriculum y del aprendizaje, un modelo pedagógico del planeamiento educacional.* Santiago, Chile: Editorial Universitaria.
Maturana, H. (2008). *The origin of humanness in the biology of love.* Exeter: Imprint Academic.
McCarthy, C. (2006). Representing the third world intellectual: C.L.R. James and the contradictory meanings of radical activism. *Anglo-Saxonica, 23*, 54–92.
Memmi, A. (1974). *The colonizer and the colonized.* London: Earthscan Publications.
Messinger, S. (1991). *La Malinche in the Mexican literature: From history to myth.* Austin, TX: University of Texas Press.
O'Gorman, E. (1995). *La invención de América.* México: Fondo de Cultura Económica.
Paz, O. (1961). *The labyrinth of solitude: Life and thought in Mexico.* New York, NY: Grove Press.
Pereira, V. P. (1980). *Paulo Freire e o nacionalismo-desenvolvimentista.* Rio de Janeiro: Civilização Brasileira.
Pinar, W. F. (2015). *Educational experience as lived: Knowledge, history, alterity.* New York, NY: Palgrave Macmillan.
Pinar, W. F. (2012). *What is curriculum theory?* New York, NY: Routledge.
Pinar, W. F. (1978). What is the reconceptualization? In W. F. Pinar (1994). *Autobiography, politics, and sexuality: Essays in curriculum theory 1972–1992* (pp. 63–72). New York, NY: Peter Lang.
Pinar, W. F. (1976). Political-spiritual dimensions. In W. F. Pinar & M. R. Grumet. *Toward a poor curriculum* (pp. 89–100). Dubuque, IA: Kendall/Hunt.
Pinar, W. F. (Ed.) (1975/2000). *Curriculum theorizing: The reconceptualization.* Troy, NY: Educator's International Press.
Pinar, W. F. (Ed.) (1974). *Heightened consciousness, cultural revolution, and curriculum theory: The proceedings of the Rochester conference.* Berkeley, CA: McCutchan Pub. Corp.
Pinar, W. F. (1973). *Sanity, madness, and the school; A phenomenological analysis of the psychological effects of 'banking' education.* Unpublished.
Pinar, W. F., Reynolds, W. M., Slattery, P., & Taubman, P. M. (Eds.) (1995). *Understanding curriculum: An introduction to the study of historical and contemporary curriculum discourses.* New York, NY: Peter Lang.
Popper, K. (1966). *The open society and its enemies.* London: Routledge.
Quijano, A. (2008). Coloniality of power, eurocentrism, and social classification. In M. Moraña, E. Dussel, & C. Jáuregui (Eds.). *Coloniality at large: Latin*

America and the postcolonial debate (pp. 513–580). Durham, NC: Duke University Press.

Ruiz, C. (2010). *De la república al mercado: Ideas educacionales y políticas en Chile*. Santiago: LOM.

Salvio, P. M. (2014). "Cities and signs": Understanding curriculum studies in Italy. In W. F. Pinar (Ed.). *International handbook of curriculum research* (2nd ed., pp. 269–277). Mahwah, NJ: Lawrence Erlbaum Associates.

Sartre, J. P. (1963). *Search for a method*. New York, NY: Knopf.

Schiefelbein, E. (1976). *Diagnóstico del sistema educacional chileno en 1970*. Santiago: Universidad de Chile.

Scholem, G. (1981). *Walter Benjamin: The story of a friendship*. Philadelphia, PA: Jewish Publication Society of America.

Schugurensky, D. (2011). *Paulo Freire*. London: Continuum International Pub. Group.

Todorov, T. (1984). *The conquest of America: The question of the other*. New York, NY: Harper & Row.

Wallerstein, I. M., (2004). *World-systems analysis: An introduction*. Durham, NC: Duke University Press.

Zemelman, M., & Jara, I. (2006). *Seis episodios de la Educación Chilena, 1920–1965*. Santiago: Ediciones de la Facultad de Filosofía y Humanidades de la Universidad de Chile.

4 The Analytical-Synthetical

During four of my five years in the Department of History at the Universidad de Concepción, I focused my study on Latin American History. I read and gathered materials for what I thought it would be the topic of my thesis:[1] Latin American popular religiosity. Many of those readings reemerged, helping to imagine this intellectual exercise. Nevertheless, I changed my mind, prompted by my experience in a class on Teaching Methodology in the Social Sciences, a class I would be a teaching assistant in the last year of my undergraduate program and my first years as a graduate student in a Master's program focused on curriculum. The academic discipline underlying that class was *Didactica de las Ciencias Sociales* [Social Sciences Didactic]. It was the combination of the subject matter and the educational approach to it that attracted me: that discipline spoke to me as a future history teacher. In that class, I was much closer to teachers' pedagogical practice than in my classes on curriculum, which were still dominated by the curriculum development paradigm and authors translated during the arrival of the field during the 1960s and early 1970s. I can say that my entry to the educational field was through the *Didactica de las Ciencias Sociales*, a specific didactic that in that tradition is generally put in tension with the general didactic as a broader educational discourse, whose place in Chile is occupied much more likely by the field of curriculum. Just graduated, I started to work in that area in teacher education. At the same time the curriculum reform that Chile had initiated some years before provided me with the opportunity to work with in-service teachers. I was also working as a schoolteacher.

It was working with my colleagues, most of them much older than me, in the professional development programs part of the curriculum reform that made me concerned with curriculum and its study. It was the turn of the century and the texts did not come from the United States but from Spain, though many were translations or these were often influenced by Anglo-Saxon literature. The scope of that literature was much wider than the one that was part of my curriculum classes just some years before (which was still at play in my former teacher education program, as I learned from youngers friends). Without abandoning the *Didactica de las Ciencias Sociales*, I started my study of curriculum that made me enroll in a Master's program with a concentration on curriculum. Even though I could not finish that program, I got far enough to have my thesis proposal approved. My idea was to apply my knowledge of Curriculum Theory, as fragmentary as it was, to the study of teacher education programs. I had the intuition that what matters in teacher education was the lived curriculum, an intuition that would be confirmed in the literature years after and that would become central to my doctoral study.

This double militancy of mine in curriculum and *Didactica Espefícica* [Specific Didactic] led me to read a book by Alicia Camillioni entitled *El Saber Didáctico* (2007) [The Didactic Knowledge]. I wanted to know more about *Didáctica General* [General Didactic] and its relation with the *Didácticas Espefícicas* and Curriculum Studies. That concern had been also prompted by students who more than once asked me "what is curriculum?" and "why do we have also didactic?" What struck me in that reading was that the same literature I had read in the field of Curriculum was referred in *El Saber Didáctico* as pertaining to the field of *Didáctica*. I believe that was my beginning on the path of thinking about academic disciplines as traditions.

In the first part of this chapter, I address the study of the U.S. educational tradition of Curriculum Studies and the *Pedagógica Latinoamericana* in their distinctiveness. This *analytical* move resonates with the historical development of both traditions that, unlike their dialogical encounter in the early 1970s, remained separated during the following decades. In the second part, I move beyond each educational tradition in its distinctiveness to address the affinities that can be found within an international conversation conceived as dialogical encounter, a *synthetical* movement. While the *analytical* moment honors distinctiveness, as opposed to exceptionality, the *synthetical* moment listens for resonances that may contribute to join together what was separately treated by analysis. Such an effort requires moving beyond ontological thinking. Distinctiveness rather than difference makes possible human understanding across traditions. In this search, Walter Benjamin's concept of elective affinities and Enrique Dussel's concept of Analectics will be my companions. Drawing on those two methodological insights, I will attempt to delineate some constellations in which elements belonging to different educational traditions can be held together. I think of this as an exploratory instance of cosmopolitan scholarship in Curriculum Studies as a worldwide field.

The Analytical: Losing Oneself Within and Without

The analogy of academic fields to countries proves fruitful when we address the need of thinking within and without a tradition. In fact, the concept of tradition challenges the spatial metaphor of a field as a country whose limits are to be kept and defended from outsiders as well as from internal enemies, usually called internationalists. It is the imagined communities suggested by identity politics that have long been part of the self-definition of any academic field and have made the classification of knowledge a canonical topic in the study of epistemology. Curriculum Studies conceived as an interdisciplinary field challenges this understanding while still struggling from within; and yet it remains trapped in its own exceptionality. Rejecting exceptionality, this first part honors distinctiveness addressing the study of the U.S. tradition of Curriculum Study and the *Pedagógica Latinoamericana*.

Loosing oneself in reading is the analytical dimension of study. In that movement one reads in a tradition, one's own or someone else's, looking for understanding from within. Therefore, abandoning for a while the international vocation of this work, I will remain within the porous borders of each tradition. This abandonment of a point of view is to some extent required by the next moment, the *synthetical*, and is certainly part of any intercultural dialogue.

The U.S. Field of Curriculum Studies

Pinar's scholarship has been informed by a focus on the study of the field of Curriculum Studies. His participation and leadership in the reconceptualization movement of the field during the 1970s and the "mapping" of the field after reconceptualization undertaken in *Understanding Curriculum* (Pinar, Reynolds, Slattery, & Taubman, 1995) are good examples of that commitment. Particularly interesting, regarding the idea of offering a synoptic view of the field, is the choice he made in *Understanding Curriculum* to report the different curriculum discourses circulating in the field after 20 years of reconceptualization rather than to synthesize one main concept to form a single point of view. The study and teaching of the field, according to Pinar, requires the intertwining of its intellectual history (vertical structure) and its current circumstances (horizontal structure). For him, these are the disciplinary structures of an academic discipline (Pinar, 2007). Understanding the field historically requires developing an intellectual history of it, an intellectual history of the field that requires "sustained attention to the external circumstances in which those ideas are formed" (Pinar, 2007, p. xiv). Pinar is drawing on Jay's concept of intellectual history, for whom intellectual history is a sort of documental study characterized by the use of "synoptic content analysis" (Pinar, 2007, p. xiv). Accordingly, to Pinar, such documentation has become a key phase in a new kind of curriculum research that allows the appreciation of the historicity of the main concepts in the field, as well as their disciplinary and personal resonance in one's intellectual project. That "is the intellectual—and pedagogical—labor of 'synoptic content analysis'" (Pinar, 2006, pp. 6–7), which enables the type of work that provides the necessary knowledge to understand the field and also to teach it. This line of work becomes crucial today when the immense amount of publications makes it difficult, if not impossible, to have a clear sense of any field's history and current circumstances. This troubling characteristic of our current academy is likely to endure, Pinar reports, given that one of today's main complaints of young scholars is the "insufficient time to study the intellectual production of their field" (Pinar, 2007, p. xii). The work of intellectual history seems of crucial importance, then.

In providing a brief historical perspective of the field of Curriculum in the United States,[2] I will follow Pinar's distinction of three main historical moments in the field's history. According to him, the American field of Curriculum Studies has faced

> three historical moments: (1) the field's inauguration and paradigmatic stabilization as curriculum development, 1918–1969; (2) the field's reconceptualization, 1969–1980, from curriculum development to [C]urriculum [S]tudies, an interdisciplinary academic field paradigmatically organized around understanding curriculum; and (3), most recently, the field's internationalization, 2000 to current.
> (Pinar, 2008, p. 495)

The first historical moment is the age of curriculum as curriculum development. This moment is characterized by the dominance of what is now known as Tyler's *rationale*. It began with Bobbitt's *The Curriculum* (1918), was consolidated by Tyler's *The Basic Principles of Curriculum and Instruction* (1949), and fell into crisis during the late 1960s (Jackson, 1968; Schwab, 1969). The common practice of locating the birth of the field of curriculum with Bobbitt is a clear indicator of the technocratic "essence" that characterized curriculum as curriculum development. However, one may ask: why is Bobbitt rather than Dewey referred to as the father of field? It is certainly a question worth asking, since Dewey was the main educational thinker in the United States and as such is a common referent in thinking curriculum in this country. Even more, looking at the use of the word curriculum, Dewey's *The Child and the Curriculum* (1902) was published 16 years before *The Curriculum* (1918). This point was made, though not fully developed, by Jackson (1992) in his historical review of the field. In spite of it, we may say that Tyler's "Principles" (1949) signals the consolidation of the field as an educational technology, given his move to tie educational objectives to evaluation.

Pinar begins his 2008 historical review in the 1950s, when the crisis of curriculum development began. To him, one of the most crucial moments for the field of curriculum in this period was the so-called Sputnik[3] crisis. This event triggered a "curricular obsession" with sciences and technology (Pinar, 2008) as necessary weapons in the mortal educational combat[4] which the United States was losing against the Soviets, in the context of the Cold War. As a consequence, science and technology would be the main content of the educational reform in the next decade—a reform in which neither teachers nor curriculum scholars, but scientists would be the main figures. That was the time in which the expression "teacher-proof reform" started to be used, as Bruner (1983) tells us, recalling his participation in that "process." As a result of this "curricular obsession," the 1960s was marked by the marginalization of curriculum scholars from curriculum reform in the United States. This marginalization "can be cited as one catalyst for the Reconceptualization of the American curriculum field in the 1970s" (Pinar et al., 1995, p. 14).

The second historical moment is the reconceptualization of the field. Reconceptualization names the move from curriculum development to curriculum understanding. It meant a paradigmatic shift "from [a] focus on social engineering and the business model to the project of understanding, which involves the concept of curriculum as conversation" (Pinar, 2004, p. 19). Consequently, an intellectually independent academic field was formed whose main purpose was understanding curriculum. This new multi-paradigmatic field was theoretically informed by work in the humanities and arts, as well as the work conducted by scholars in Gender and African-American studies. The reconceptualization of the field since the mid-1970s sought to understand curriculum "historically, politically, racially, autobiographically or biographically, aesthetically, theologically, institutionally and internationally, as well as in terms of gender, phenomenology, postmodernism, and poststructuralism" (Pinar, 2008, p. 493). The field emerging from that process was that *Understanding Curriculum* mapped in the mid-1990s. "The dying patient[5] on which Schwab, Huebner, and Pinar commented from 1969 to 1978 has been profoundly revived due to the transfusions of important ideas from other fields" (Pinar et al., 1995, p. 849) and continents. At that time the field had been not just reconceptualized but had also become international.

The third historical moment of the field is its internationalization. This process was already announced in *Curriculum Understanding* (Pinar et al., 1995), but it became a visible reality at the turn of the century, when the first *International Conference for the Advancement of Curriculum Studies* took place in Louisiana in 2001. That was the occasion for the foundation of the *International Association for the Advancement of Curriculum Studies*. The main proceedings of that conference were published in the volume *Internationalization of Curriculum Studies* (Trueit, 2003). According to Pinar, the internationalization of Curriculum Studies "promises deepened understanding of the local and the individual through encounters with the global and the collective" (Pinar, 2008, p. 502). The present text is the result of some of those encounters.

This view of the history of the field must not, however, be understood linearly; the complexity that intertwines the horizontal and vertical structure of the field is not to be forgotten. These three "historical" moments (curriculum development, reconceptualization, and internationalization) are temporal divides but also conceptual perspectives. The *analytical* need to situate them temporally in order to tell the history must not lead us to forget that these three "moments" coexist today with great complexity. Curriculum development or curriculum design is a key component of current educational reform as well as part of the daily practice of teaching, and not just in schools. Most of the work initially addressed by the reconceptualists is now a part of the mainstream in the field (subfield) of Curriculum Theory and Curriculum History. Internationalization is also an integral part of the field's concerns both in the United States and around the world. Connecting the past, the present, and the future is then an important task in any effort to understand the field of curriculum.

Understanding the field in its current circumstances is the task of the horizontal disciplinary structure. In this regard, Pinar (2007) reminds us that, horizontality "refers not only to the field's present circumstances . . . as well as the social and political milieus which influence, and so often, structure this set" (p. xiv). Therefore, at beginning of the first decades of the twenty-first century, curriculum is an "interdisciplinary academic field devoted to understanding curriculum" (Pinar, 2011, p. ix), "a divergent field moving in multiple directions" (Pinar, 2011, p. 123). The latter is internally the main disciplinary challenge of its present moment of Curriculum Studies. The capability of "talking across" and among particulars is more necessary than ever, regarding the centripetal forces acting in this divergent field. We can see that in Pinar's call for the reconstruction of the field by addressing his intellectual legacy is an example of how horizontality and verticality are intertwined disciplinary structures. To Pinar (2007), intellectual history and the reconstruction of the canon as a bibliographical statement of the intellectual legacy of the field could provide "disciplinary infrastructure" for its advancement. This, however, is not an easy task in a field that; reconceptualized, became also anti-canonical. Paradoxically, or not, today the larger field of education characterized by the culture of presentism tends to make more urgent the necessity for the field to become historical.

More than two decades has passed from the publication of *Curriculum Understanding: An Introduction to the Study of Historical and Contemporary Curriculum Discourses* (Pinar et al., 1995)—a book conceived as an introduction to the study of historical and contemporary curriculum written discourses through listening to "what the field was saying" (p. xiv) in its "cacophony of voices" (p. xiii). While successfully reporting the internal situation of a field nurtured by interdisciplinary and foreign scholarship during the decades that preceded its appearance, *Curriculum Understanding* was also an effort to become historical. Therefore, it addressed those landscapes not just in an effort to overcome the atheoretical trait of Curriculum Studies but also its ahistorical one. *Curriculum Understanding* finishes with a word to the next generation: "What the next generation might explore is a political phenomenological understanding of curriculum, influenced by gender analysis, autobiographical theory, situated internationally in a multiracial global village" (Pinar et al., 1995, p. 864). While Pinar's scholarship focused in the following decades on the internationalization of the field, both its development and study, at the turning of the second decade of this century he came back to look at the field of Curriculum Studies in the United States. This work will occupy our attention in the first part of this chapter.

Curriculum as a "complicated conversation" is now threatened by an educational context constrained by objectives and guidelines and overdetermined by outcomes. In that context curriculum struggles to remain conversational in the midst of the deliberate destruction of public education (Pinar, 2012, 2011, 2004). This is the result of the social engineering obsession that believes finding the right technique, organization, practice, students, teachers, standards, or research will allow students to learn what a teacher teaches them. For a field marginalized by school reform a half century ago, to witness this "nightmare" that is the present, Pinar (2013) writes, "there must be profound frustration and, if not self-blame, then at least some degree of self-dissociation" (p. 3). As in the 1960s, the current constructed crisis of education serves to move the guilt from politicians and economists to teachers and teacher educators. The discourses of school reform situates education, not politics (civilian and military) and the economy, as the place in which the nation is put at risk by letting children slip behind the standards and not providing the labor force required for success in the global economy. Therefore, "school reform is a political reenactment of that repetition-compulsion characteristic of posttraumatic behavior" (Pinar, 2012, p. 65). The past is in the present, its intellectual history and present circumstances, in their affinities.

Pinar's main work in this endeavor is *Curriculum Studies in the United States: Present Circumstances and Intellectual Histories* (Pinar, 2013). The "U.S. field's external circumstances today are not entirely different from those in 1970 when Joseph Schwab asserted that the field was moribund. The internal circumstances of the field are quite different" (Pinar, 2013, p. 9). Thus, Pinar affirms, the external circumstances are currently not very different from those of the late 1960s and early 1970s, namely a "national" context marked by educational reform informed by instrumental rationality. This corresponds today to the "deliberate destruction of public education" (Pinar, 2013, p. 3), the "culture of competition" (Pinar, 2013, p. 18), the "obsession with test scores" (Pinar, 2013, p. 20), and so on. In reenactment of school reform, Curriculum scholars are not now replaced by scientists as then but by economists. These are "left alone to ask the crucial curriculum question: *what knowledge is of most worth?*" (Pinar, 2013, p. 20). Then, when faced with the necessary failure, the blame is put on public schools and teachers. Pinar (2013) continues:

> Playing *exactly* the same scapegoating card that politicians had used after the 1957 Sputnik satellite launching (Pinar, 2012, pp. 102–104)

and again in the early 1980s—then with the 1983 publication of *A Nation at Risk* (Pinar, 2012, pp. 200–202)—former Secretary of State Condoleezza Rice and the former chancellor of New York City's schools, Joel I. Klein, warned in March 2012 that the nation's security and economic prosperity are at risk if schools fail to improve.

(p. 29)

While this school "deform" (Pinar, 2012) continues to define the external circumstances of the field of curriculum in the United States, the internal circumstances of this field are quite different from those when Schwab (1969) pronounced the field moribund, Pinar claims. Four decades of reconceptualization have changed the field's scholarship. Nevertheless, the main concepts that informed this process seem to be close to their point of exhaustion. The exhaustion of concepts such as power, identity, and discourse, Pinar remarks, is not "criticism but, rather, acknowledgement of their success" (Pinar, 2013, p. 10). They are broadly shared across the field to the point that rather than being conceptual innovations, they enjoy a taken-for-grantedness. Pinar elaborates:

> As assumptions, these concepts circulate as accepted truth—even the poststructuralist truth that there is no truth!—and have thus become abstractions split off from the concrete complexity of the historical moment. Split off, they do not link us to the present and can no longer provide passages to the future. In their triumph they become markers of our defeat: our expulsion from the public sphere.
>
> (Pinar, 2013, p. 11)

I believe this expulsion from the public sphere, namely public education, by and through school reform is not unrelated to the self-reflective process that characterized the field's reconceptualization in the United States as a process of *concientizing*. Through this academic trauma Curriculum Studies became an academic field in the field of education. Within the latter, as a field colonized by other academic fields such as psychology, sociology, economics, and so on, Curriculum Studies became an interdisciplinary educational field. Is it that through/by its own estrangement Curriculum Studies found itself? This is not to say that curriculum rejects, or should reject, any theoretical influence coming from those colonizing fields. On the contrary, Curriculum Studies is already an academic field characterized by an interdisciplinary distinctiveness. Furthermore, what we know today as Curriculum Studies is a field nurtured by interdisciplinary dialogue. And yet Curriculum Studies remains an educational discourse in the field of education.

The field's intellectual history seems to be useful to understand this emphasis on power as an explanatory category during the 1970s. Not surprisingly, after "the resounding defeat of 1968" (Pinar, 2013, p. 44), they made race and gender their tributary concepts in the effort to understand curriculum as a political text. Internally, the concept of power was a fruitful tool against the proceduralism of the so-called Tyler rationale. Therefore, Pinar explains, "the concept of race declared its sovereignty with the publication of Cameron McCarthy's 1990 *Race and Curriculum*" (Pinar, 2013, p. 45). In spite of its distinctiveness, historically and terminologically speaking, the concept of power became also central in other curriculum discourses such as those that aim to understand curriculum as a gendered text. Now, however, "these concepts threaten to annul agency by collectivizing identity and totalizing power, erasing the singularity of students and teachers who can now only be construed as "conduits" of economic or racialized or gendered reproduction" (Pinar, 2013, p. 49).

Alongside power, the following decades saw an increasing usage of the concepts of identity and discourse as analytical categories in curriculum scholarship. It was not out of the blue that *Curriculum Understanding* (1995) conceived the different "voices" in the field as "texts" or "discourses." Regardless of the richness that these concepts brought to the field's work, the efforts to "understand curriculum as postmodern, poststructuralist, and deconstructed text also face the conceptual exhaustion that comes with their success" (Pinar, 2013, p. 49). As important as these categories—power, identity, analysis—were in the field's history, given its external and internal circumstances, now

> because these discourses have become widely accepted they are now ingrained in the mainstream assumptions of the U.S. field. To assert them as somehow still "new" requires their endless radicalization, stretching them from provocative insight into a specific situation into a nomological law that is everywhere and always true, even when that "law" decrees there are no laws.
> (Pinar, 2013, p. 49)

Therefore, the concepts, that "once reconceptualized the U.S. field—power, identity, and discourse—appear to have played themselves out, signaled by tendencies toward totalization, reductionism and self-referentiality" (Pinar, 2013, p. 49). According to Pinar, this heritage of the reconceptualization process is at the center of its present moving on to the next moment. This calls for the burdensome work, according to him, which is a labor of rereferentialization since the main concepts in the field have become dereferentialized, namely that they are no longer able to enunciate the present moment, "itself simultaneously unprecedented and utterly familiar" (Pinar, 2013, p. 66).

Nevertheless, the present circumstances of the field today are not just the external hostility and the internal conceptual exhaustion of its main concepts. A third component is also part of the Curriculum Studies' present circumstances: internationalization. Pinar writes:

> Within present circumstances—1) debilitating hostility externally, including the destruction of the field's historic object of scholarship: the public school, 2) conceptual exhaustion as the key concepts (power, discourse, identity) fade from the foreground into background assumptions, and 3) internationalization—a third paradigmatic moment struggles to start in the U.S.
>
> (Pinar, 2013, p. 53)

Accordingly, the rereferentialization that Pinar calls for is to define a process in which "concepts from other disciplines, countries, cultural traditions, and historical moments enable us to enunciate the present moment" (Pinar, 2013, p. 66). Thus, internationalization seems to have a major role in the renovation of the field, just as has been historically the case. This process must not be thought of as a matter of exploitation but of self-excavation, a concept that articulates the search without thematizing the destination (Pinar, 2013). Pinar elaborates:

> By juxtaposing present circumstances and intellectual histories, I am underscoring that we must "work through" the present, not instrumentalize our way "forward." The future is elsewhere, in both historical and geographical terms. Supplementing the solidarity that the old Communist concept "internationalism" promised, internationalization singularizes our situation by requiring that self-understanding we aspire to communicate to others as we inhabit the "commons" that is the field worldwide.
>
> (Pinar, 2013, p. 52)

In Pinar's scholarship, internationalization is seen to have an important role to play in what he calls the next moment of the field, "providing both conceptual distance from the U.S. field's present circumstances and intellectual histories, as well as provocations for reconstructing the canon and formulating new concepts" (Pinar, 2013, p. 7). This is to say that internationalization may enable a cosmopolitan reenactment of the field's character, moving it from "the disabling provincialism accompanying American conceptions of their exceptionality" (Pinar, 2013, pp. 7–8). Study is the key term that enables this process in a field whose character in the second decade of the twentieth century remains a project under construction. This study requires attention to the field's legacy. The call for internationalization is not a call for forgetting but for memory.

> No one works from a blank slate. No single, even canonical, concept—alignment with society (Bobbitt) or society's reconstruction through

human intelligence (Dewey), curriculum development through protocol (Tyler), curriculum practice as deliberation (Schwab), curriculum for the sake of transcendence (Huebner), and humanization (Macdonald)—solves the disciplinary problem of the present moment, a divergent field moving in multiple directions. Together, these historic concepts form a rich and dynamic intellectual legacy from which we can continue to reconstruct the US field, working through its atheoretical, ahistorical imprinting one hundred years ago.

(Pinar, 2011, p. 123)

Furthermore, Pinar tells us, study is a concept that "signals the significance of specific traditions of those who were first identified" with cosmopolitanism. He sees the model of Torah study, affirming the intersection of present circumstances and intellectual histories, as a model in which "U.S. scholars can undertake the reconceptualization of curriculum studies" (Pinar, 2013, pp. 7–8). It is interesting that Pinar's insistence on study connects his search to the Semitic tradition. This was also the intuition of Dussel in his effort to develop a Latino American thinking beyond Eurocentrism, which placed the subcontinent outside of history. Even more, the primacy of ethics rather than politics in the field resonates with the *Pedagógica Latinoamericana*, which was first developed within the ethic of Latino American liberation. In the next section, I will address the *Pedagógica Latinoamericana* in its distinctiveness.

The Pedagógica Latinoamericana

The *Pedagógica Latinoamericana* has a major figure in the Latin American pedagogue Paulo Freire. Freire's main books carry in their title the word *pedagogía*, pedagogy in English. As Freire understood it, *pedagogía* does not preoccupy itself with which methods are the best to guarantee educational learning but with thinking that reflects upon the Latin American praxis of liberation and its educational implications. The *Pedagógica Latinoamericana* is a moment of the Latin American thinking of liberation, particularly of the philosophy of liberation. In this part of the chapter, I focus on the *Pedagógica Latinoamericana* as it was developed by Enrique Dussel. His usage of the word *pedagógica* instead of *pedagogía* is intended to suggest the theoretical, philosophical, nature of his work. Given that this work is barely known among Anglo-American audiences, I concentrate on the main works by Dussel written during the early 1970s and 1980s, even though I will also follow his most recent publications. I will address first the *Pedagógica Latinoamericana* as focused on the symbolic, to move then to the critique of the ontology of modernity as educational project, and finish with its affirmative moment, namely a pedagogy of liberation, or liberating education. In Dussel's words the path goes from the symbolic, to the dialectic, to the analectic.

The Pedagógica Latinoamericana as a Pedagogical Symbolic

This was a Latin American reinterpretation (*reconceptualization* was also a term at use then) of the main academic disciplines such as sociology, theology, philosophy. It was made possible by the opening of a new horizon of meaning that follows reflection upon *Latinoamérica* and its distinctiveness. The search was first historical. That was the origin of dependency theory, for example, whose first historiographical developments preceded by almost one decade its economic ones. The humanities also addressed this historical turn, thus becoming historical, reflecting on Latin American history and its symbols (Dussel, 2013). The Latino American boom in literature provided the works of imagination in which many of these symbols were to be found. The philosophy of liberation, first articulated as an ethic of Latin American Liberation, used these materials to elaborate the main Latin American dialectic: domination-liberation. At the center was the European invasion that began in 1492, the primal phenomenon of modernity. The *Pedagógica Latinoamericana* also followed this path.

> An Ontological ethics is properly *dialectics*. A metaphysical ethics is originally *analectics*. Ethic begins thus from a *symbolic*, which it thinks *dialectically* and questions *analectically*; moving from existential ethic to ontological ethic, and from there, through the mediation of trans-existential, to metaphysical ethic.
>
> (Dussel, 1973a, p. 125)

Therefore, the Lain American tradition puts at the front of its educational reflection an ethics that goes beyond the logic of identity, responding to the interpellation of the *Otro*. The *Pedagógica Latinoamericana* begins by focusing on the educational process that followed the military and erotic domination that was the conquest. The *mestizo* appears as a dialectical image, which can help us to unfold its problematic. Since the *mestizos* are neither Spanish nor *indio*, they "live in their own flesh the contradictory tension of modernity as both emancipation and sacrificial myth" (Dussel, 1995, p. 125). The *mestizo* born from the erotic domination of his *india* mother becomes also the object of the pedagogical domination of his European father. Her father is the male conqueror, ergo his oppressor, who unfolds himself into the dominating educator. Dussel (1980) quotes Bartolome de Las Casas affirming that "commonly, wars do not let alive other than youngsters and women" (p. 18). The latter will become the raped mothers of the *mestizo* race—children that are the beginning of a new pedagogical style, Dussel concludes. The *mestizo* is the child of the *Pedagógica Latinoamericana*.

Dussel (1980) continues affirming that "the orphan *per excellentia* of this *pedagogics* of domination is not any child but the mainly the child from the periphery" (p. 16); it is a colonial and neocolonial orphan. This is to say that the *mestizo latinoamericano* is a rude barbarian needing to be educated into civilization, but the Latin Americano child is not confirmed as *mestizo* but negated in its distinctiveness having to deny his *india* mother. To Dussel this expresses the need, posed by the pedagogy of domination, to negate the popular culture in favor of the higher culture of the empire or the nation state. The reenactments of the Empire's civilizing project by the new republics during the centuries that followed the *independencia latinoamericana* have failed to affirm *mestizos*' double origin, without discovering their *indio* and *negro* heritages.

> That is the paradoxical position of the *Latin American* child: the incapacity to accept the originary domination of the strongest, his father—the imperial state first, and the neocolonial one after—betraying his own culture that breastfed him with its symbols alongside the original milk.
>
> (Dussel, 1980, p. 16)

What is required is a pedagogy that enables the *mestizo* to surpass the historical trauma of the conquest and subsequent colonization, and of slavery that has "left indelible marks and demands a deep practical and theoretical, ethical, cultural and economic-political transformation of the alterity excluded for centuries" (p. 183). To move beyond this original denial of the *Otro* is for the *mestizo latinoamericano* a task of historical reconstruction, a reconstruction that begins with the reciprocal respect of a dialogical encounter. This reciprocal respect enables the beginning of a pedagogy of liberation that goes beyond the world that is given to him and her. This is the affirmative moment of the *Pedagógica Latinoamericana* that not only negates the pedagogy of domination of the present but also creates the future. To the *Pedagógica Latinoamericana*, the *mestizo latinoamericano* must affirm his and her dual character, beginning with his and her mother's heritage but acknowledging also his father's. This is not only a matter of negation of the negation but also of the affirmative moment of personal and collective reconstruction. For *Latinoamérica* as a *mestizo continent*, its reconstruction requires a pedagogy of liberation.

The Critique of Modernity

Like the field of Curriculum Studies, the *Pedagógica Latinoamericana* is highly symbolic. The *Pedagógica Latinoamericana* continues as a criticism of the ontology of modernity, which has the father, the imperial state, and the preceptor as the main subjects of its pedagogy. The father-state-teacher is in fact the reenactment of the *cogito ergo sum*, deployed as well as announced first by the *conquero ergo sum*, and then it becomes *doceo ergo sum*. This modern pedagogy was born out of the praxis of domination constitutive of the European subject, having its first performance in the conquest and colonization of what we now call *América*. Against this pedagogy, coming out of the primal phenomenon of modernity, the *Pedagógica Latinoamericana* focused on the face-to-face of the intergenerational relationships. The child is not an orphan, he has his parents who, as his first proximity, are able to establish a dialogical relation. Thus, a pedagogical face-to-face is a passage between the erotics to the politics and it is both continuous and overlooked (Dussel, 1980). The *Pedagógica Latinoamericana* understands education as a liminal space.

> The child born in the home is educated in order to form part of a political community; the child born in a culture is expected to find a home. That is why pedagogical discourse is always twofold, and the planes continually become confused. This matter has been more or less well stated in what is called the "second Oedipus complex." The young man in his adolescence again situates himself in an oedipal conflict, but now in a socio-psychoanalytical context. The pulsion toward the mother is at the same time toward the ancestral, the popular culture; the interposition of the father is likewise that of society or the state. His "ego ideal" (father-state) is in crisis. The young man cannot identify with a decadent imago patris; the oedipal conflict persists, and its revelation is youthful rebellion as a symptom of sexual and political repression.
> (Dussel, 1985, p. 87)

The *Pedagógica Latinoamericana* occupies itself with the intergenerational transmission of accumulated culture through pedagogical systems. "The educational system and the mass media are today the two most important systems in the formation of the average person" (Dussel, 1985, p. 88). These systems are usually "patriarchal, where the male dominates the female and the couple dominates the child. This pedagogical system is erotically uxoricidal and pedagogically filicidal" (Dussel, 1985, p. 88). To Dussel, the worldwide events of 1968 are a generational rejection of the filicide, being sadly a new filicide. He elaborates:

> That rebellion of the child against the gerontocracies (elders) and the bureaucracies, not only of the neocolonial bourgeoisie, but also against the opulence society, the destruction of society, and consumption of societies of multinational corporations; produces a new filicide, a tragic moment of the *Pedagógica Latinoamericana*.
> (Dussel, 1980, p. 23)

That is for the Latin American philosopher the meaning of 1968, the *Tlatelolco* massacre. The negation of the child's exteriority is expressed in the negation of his/her material life. It is beyond the system where the erotic-political-pedagogical exteriority is to be found and continues to live. The child is the exteriority of the erotics, he "is the other from whom one always has to learn how to listen in silence to the new revelation that is brought to past history as tradition" (Dussel, 1985, p. 88). Moreover, since the pedagogical space is a passage between the erotic and the political, the child is also a political-pedagogical exteriority. "The child, the new one, is not an orphan," as modernity pretends, but "the offspring of its parents and of a people" (Dussel, 1985, p. 89). Otherwise, what follows is a filicide, the cultural death of the child. The denial of the child's exteriority by the pedagogical system is commonly done in the name of his freedom and well-being, and by the deployment of the best pedagogical methods at hand. The *Pedagógica Latinoamericana* reads the canonical texts of modern pedagogy, such as Rousseau's *Emile*, against the grain. Dussel writes:

> The preceptor (the father or the state) obliges the pupil to be or to behave like an orphan (without mother and hence without popular culture) and to be obedient in everything, as Rousseau explains in *Emile*. Claiming that nature expresses itself in reality, the repressing preceptor obliges Emile to follow a fixed curriculum tenaciously in order to merit his title of petit bourgeois, with even a European tour (the delight of the bourgeoisie of the time) and with a perfectly docile wife, a repressed housewife.
> (Dussel, 1985, pp. 90–91)

School as pedagogical-political institution, alongside the other pedagogical systems, shapes as well as imprisons the child. Unlike this pedagogy, the *Pedagógica Latinoamericana* aims at the child's liberation. It is, thus, metaphysical since it goes beyond the world as given allowing the son and the daughter to be as *Otro*. In Dussel's words, to "allow the son to be, so that Oedipus grows as another, as the anti-Oedipus, is to respect him in his [and her] exteriority" (Dussel, 1985, p. 92). This enables a praxis of pedagogical liberation, which is also erotic as well as political. The Malinche's child as an *Otro* must be an anti-Emile that is not let alone before its preceptor having to accept what is given, but situating itself in the continuity-discontinuity of a tradition.

A Pedagogy of Liberation

A path of reconstruction starts by working through the past. Recognizing the child's exteriority the pedagogy of liberation is an anti-pedagogy of the pedagogy of domination. The project of domination within modern education annihilates what is otherness, namely the new generation, the oppressed populations, the peripheral cultures; the project of liberation emphasizes the *Otro*'s exteriority—the student's, the oppressed's, the peripheral's.

> The ethos of pedagogical liberation demands that the teacher know how to listen with respect in silence to youth, to the people. Only the genuine teacher who has become a patient and enthusiastic disciple can attain an adequate discernment of the reality in which a people finds itself. Pupils, the young, and the people admire teachers who, in their lifestyle, in their living together with them, in their humility and service, dedicate a critical awareness to affirming the values inherent in the young and in the people. Such teachers manifest a collaboration that unifies, mobilizes, organizes, and creates.
> (Dussel, 1985, p. 94)

We are now in the affirmative moment of the *Pedagógica Latinoamericana*. There is no magisterial ego before which an orphaned entity must passively wait to be taught, but a fountain-like exteriority of what is not yet. In this tradition the educational face-to-face is crucially played in the bipolarity word-ear, as an interpellation-listening relationality in Levinasian terms. Then, the welcoming what is not-me becomes service to the other as *Otro*.

The disciple is new history. The liberating-liberated father-teacher-state listens to this new history that reveals the child's exteriority and allows the child to be not from the paternal-maternal project, which is also educational and political, but from the filial project. This metaphysical project is revealed before the silent attentive mother-teacher-state. The *Pedagógica Latinoamericana* is a pedagogy of listening, a pedagogy of silence.

This pedagogy of listening is crucial in Freire's work. To the *Pedagógica Latinoamericana*, the *Otro* is worthy to be listened to. In this pedagogy of listening the son and the daughter are also fully human and able to communicate. As *Otro*, the disciple is exteriority to the adult totality and the possibility of a renewal of life. He is the not-yet of his progenitor. Her mere presence speaks future. Dussel (1980) writes, "The pedagogical face-to-face, then, is respect for the *Otro*, . . . the sacred before which no love is sufficient, no hope excessive, and no faith adequate" (p. 150). Therefore, the disciple is no longer an orphan in need of paternal authority, remaining silent before his or her father-teacher-government. On the contrary, he or she is to be listened to. "It is necessary to be silent before what cannot be talked: the revelation of the *Otro* as other, as a mystery, as distinct. "His/her" revelation is "inexpressible" (*Unaussprechliches*) from "my" [our] world" (Dussel, 1980, p. 92). In silence, one awaits for the revelation of the *Otro*. It is in that silence that we honor the *Otro*'s distinctiveness. It is in the dialogical engagement that follows that humanity may be revealed as an analogical species. This tension between distinctiveness and commonality by analogy resonates in the tension between the *analytical* and the *synthetical* moments of *currere*.

The Synthetical: A Work in Elective Affinities

The *synthetical* is an affirmative moment. It is the attempt to reconstruct oneself, including one's intellectual influences. As said earlier, while the *analytical* focuses on the distinctiveness of each tradition, the *synthetical* moment listens for resonances. The *synthetical* is a work in elective affinities. Defining the concept of elective affinities, I explore its methodological potential in looking for correspondences among the traditions just analyzed in their distinctiveness, namely the Anglo-American Curriculum Studies and the *Pedagógica Latinoamericana*. Later, I use the same concept to describe a field of correspondences between *currere* and *Bildung*. I finish by connecting this work of elective affinities with the idea of cosmopolitanism since it is the dialogical encounter of educational tradition in their analogical distinctiveness that makes possible a more comprehensive theory of education.

Elective Affinity

Elective affinity (*Wahlverwandschaften*) is a useful concept to describe a constellation that becomes visible only when signaled, making clear how disparate elements acquire a form. The form that such a constellation takes presupposes a certain attraction among its elements that holds them together in a given disposition. Thus, I believe elective affinity to be a powerful concept to study the correspondences between two intellectual projects that do not necessarily inform each other, yet seem related. The idea of a field of correspondences is the first level of elective affinities. A correspondence, at that level, refers to a "spiritual relationship, a structural homology" (Löwy, 1992, p. 11), a "network of analogies, similitudes, or equivalences among several elements" (Löwy, 1992, p. 21) of two or more bodies of scholarship; or two or more educational traditions in our case.

Elective Affinity is first the title of a novel by Goethe and second, the title of Benjamin's critical essay on Goethe's work, an essay that Benjamin considered an exemplary criticism. It is there that the novelty of the concept must be found. Originally, the term refers to a chemical (alchemical) feature of certain materials that allow them to combine with different degrees of fusion. The concept was also used by Weber to describe the *wahlverwandschaften* between capitalism and Protestant ethics. More recently, Michael Löwy (1992) has used the concept to describe a sort of magnetic field "polarized by libertarian romanticism and Jewish messianism" (p. 3). He writes: "starting from a certain structural analogy, the relation consists of a convergence, a mutual attraction, an active confluence, a combination that can go as far as a fusion" (p. 6). This concept, Löwy suggests, "enable[s] us to understand (in the strong sense of *verstehen*) a certain kind of connection between seemingly disparate phenomena within the same cultural field" (p. 10). Those connections are named by Löwy as "a very special kind of dialectical relationship" (Löwy, 1992, p. 6). While I agree with Löwy in his interest in building "on the methodological status of the concept as an interdisciplinary research tool," I believe this methodological status has the potential of going beyond dialectics, or at least to a reconciliation of this with analogy. The expression "elective affinities" foresees a possible intimate union of disparate elements. This is the work of possibilities brought about by criticism.

Drawing on Benjamin's concept of criticism conceived as "an infinite process of supplementation" (Gilloch, 2002, p. 35) moves from what is already in a work in order to complement it. Quoting Novalis, Benjamin asserts "the true reader must be the extended author". The writer, Freire would add, "gets to know, to interact with, the distant readers who probably will read the book when he or she is no longer in existence . . . , facing them symbolically" (Freire & Shor, 1987, p. 2). This ceaseless excavation in the texts is at the center of an intellectual work dealing with the afterlife of texts—as material cultural practices. Cultural criticism completes the work of the intellectual imagination.

This is, at least to some extent, the project contained in the work of the Latin American thinking of liberation at a methodological level. This reflection, present from the beginning in the Latin American tradition, revives in a human and educational context marked by planetary agony. This is not to say that dialectical thinking must be ignored or negated, but subsumed into a methodological device that enables intercultural dialogue across different traditions. That is the potential of the Latin American Analectical, which begins by claiming the "analectical moment opens us to the metaphysical sphere . . . referring us to the other" (Dussel, 1985, p. 158). The Levinasian category of exteriority remains useful at this methodological level, adding an affirmative moment to the useful yet insufficient negative dialectics. It subsumes negative dialectics, ergo the logic of identity into a non-coincidence space.

> The analectical moment is the affirmation of exteriority; it is not only the denial of the denial of the system from the affirmation of the totality. It is the overcoming of totality but not only as the actuality of what is in potency in the system. It is the overcoming of totality from internal transcendentality from exteriority that has never been within. To affirm exteriority is to realize what is impossible for the system (there being no potency for it); it is to realize the new, what has not been foreseen by the totality, that which arises from freedom that is unconditioned, revolutionary, innovative.
>
> (Dussel, 1985, p. 160)

The acknowledgement of non-coincidence, of an "irrespective relationship" (Dussel, 1973a, p. 127), is the ground from which the new becomes a possibility for transformation of the present. Furthermore, the analectical, methodologically speaking, enables the study of educational traditions dialogically. In this sense, it is closer to the device of *currere* as allegory (Pinar, 2012, pp. 49–52), used by Pinar (2013), "to underscore the utterly unique and decidedly common character of our circumstances" (p. 66), a Benjaminian concept fruitful for a work of elective affinities through which new constellations can be heard.

First Constellation: Curriculum Studies and the Pedagógica Latinoamericana

> Curriculum is a complicated conversation. This fundamental fact acknowledges not only the individuality and situatedness of students and teachers, but also of those whose works they study. It implies, as education did for Walter Benjamin, "the immanent unity of knowledge," as well as "non-hierarchical relations between teachers and students and between males and females in the university community at large." Not only organizational, such a conception called for students´ commitment to "unceasing spiritual revolution" as well as "radical doubt" that could create "the culture of conversation."
>
> (Pinar, 2015, p. 109)

> Human existence cannot be Silent, nor can it be nourished by false words, but only by true words, with which men and women transform the world. To exist, humanly, is to name the world, to change it. Once named, the world in its turn reappears to the namers as a problem and requires of them a new naming. Human beings are not built in silence, but in word, in work, in action-reflection.
>
> (Freire, 1970, p. 88)

Having Paulo Freire as its major figure, the relation between the *Pedagógica Latinoamericana* and the field of Curriculum Studies was already established in the foundational moment of what was named the reconceptualization of the U.S. field. At that moment, resonances with continental thought, such as psychoanalysis, existentialism, and phenomenology, are to be found in both traditions. That same background put into relation with the intellectual history of the authors of those traditions, help them to perform the critique of instrumental perspectives in education. Furthermore, what is suggested now is about work to come, since the intellectual history of the Latin American educational tradition has not been written, although the works cited in this writing show that the project is underway.

The Primacy of Ethics

The necessary primacy of ethics in education is increasingly alluded to across educational traditions. To the *Pedagógica Latinoamericana*, this primacy is part of the foundational texts of the Latin American thinking of liberation in both of its main venues: theology of liberation and philosophy of liberation. The *Pedagógica Latinoamericana* was first developed in the early 1970s in *Hacia una Etica de la Liberación Latinoamericana* [Towards an Ethics of the Latin American Liberation] (Dussel, 1973a, 1973b). It was Dussel's recontextualization of Levinas's category of *L'autre* [the Other] and *l'Extériorité* [Exteriority] that announced the birth of the Latin American ethic of liberation. As for Levinas, ethics is for Dussel "first philosophy." Dussel writes,

> Thanks to a lecture by another Jewish philosopher—Levinas—who we met in Paris in the 60s (alongside Sartre and Ricoeur), we were able to overcome the narrow understanding of ontological Totality that dominated Critical Theory from Horkheimer to Marcuse, Apel, and Habermas. In *Totality and Infinity: An Essay on Exteriority*, "the Other" (Altrui) was the "poor" (economically other), the "widow" (erotically other), the "orphan" (pedagogically other), the "foreigner" (politically other), etc. These were the multiple faces of alterity.
>
> (Dussel, 2011, pp. 17–18)

The concrete faces of alterity must be put at the center of our concerns with injustice, inequality, and self-reification. In Curriculum Studies, internationalization emerges "as the ethical engagement of alterity" (Pinar, 2014, p. 524). These ethical problems of our present follow from "freezing the fluidity of the historical present into apparently timeless structures resistant to reconstruction" (Pinar, 2012, p. 131), requiring the field to become historical. Pinar (2011) juxtaposes Marx's and Kierkegaard's works to speak of a historical consciousness that enables taking responsibility of the present. In that move, Pinar recalls the critique of Hegel conducted by the post-Hegelians:

> It was Friedrich Wilhelm Joseph Schelling, Toews (2004, p. 420) reports, who provided the provocation for Marx and Kierkegaard's analyses. At his inaugural lecture—presented at the University of Berlin on November 15, 1841—Schelling presented himself as a "teacher of the age" (Toews, 2004, p, 1). "I feel the full significance of this moment," Schelling told those assembled; "I know what responsibilities I have taken upon myself" (quoted in Toews, 2004, p. 1). At age 66, Toews (2004, p. 2) continues, Schelling understood himself as the "living embodiment" of a "philosophy of freedom," in which historically attuned action in the present discloses the future. Schelling criticized the self-enclosing and totalizing structure of Hegel's philosophy, its "conflation" of "being" with what is (2004, 6).
>
> (Pinar, 2011, p. 129)

This same reference to the post-Hegelians, and specifically to Schelling's Berlin lectures of 1841 is to be found in Dussel's scholarship. Reading

Schelling, he affirms, "we have found the origin of our own work" (Dussel, 1974. p. 122). It was Schelling that offered to Dussel to take his reflection "beyond the dialectical ontology of identity, of being and thinking, there is the possibility of the unthinkable" (Dussel, 1973b, p. 157). This is at the center of Dussel's analectical ethic, whose concrete exemplar is Freire's pedagogy, which for Dussel signals the emergence of an ethical-critical-consciousness. Freire articulates, Dussel (2013) says,

> a planetary pedagogy that aims to make ethical-critical consciousness emerge. He is concerned not only with the cognitive or the affective improvement (of social victims among others) but also with the production of an ethical-critical consciousness. This ethical-critical consciousness originates in the victims themselves by virtue of their being the privileged historical subjects of their own liberation. The critical pedagogical act is performed by the subjects themselves and in their transforming praxis: liberation is thus the "place" and the "purpose" of this pedagogy.
>
> (Dussel, 2013, p. 321)

Freire's ethical-critical-consciousness is a result of a dialogical encounter, an "analectical unity of two moments: the voice-of-the-Other and the open ear of the totality" (Dussel, 1973b, p. 57). It is through this experience that subjective and social reconstruction is possible. Curriculum Studies must have ethics as its centerpiece, aware that "while structural noncoincidence [exteriority] provides the opportunity for subjective reconstruction, that undertaking occurs in specific material and temporal conditions" (Pinar, 2012, p. 135). In the same sense, in thinking of intercultural dialogue across educational traditions, the centrality of ethics seems unmistakably correct. This intercultural dialogue requires one to study both one's own intellectual history and present circumstances and also to study the others' study of their own.

Pinar suggests that study must be also be recovered as an important companion in curriculum. Interestingly, the field of curriculum has already found this in naming the field: Curriculum Studies. Addressing the concept of study itself, Pinar follows Block (2004), to whom study is an ethic, a way of being. Block empathizes also with the religious grounds of the word study that he connects to the Jewish tradition. Pinar (2013) sees in that tradition, specifically in the model of the Torah study, a path to the U.S. Curriculum Studies field's rejuvenation.

Study

The concept of study has also been used by the *Pedagógica Latinoamericana* to refer to scholarship and research. Dussel (1973a) opposes the concept of study to forgetting, which is a form of knowledge too; study produces remembering. And, like the work of remembrance, study is a difficult task, one that, according to Freire in his *The Act of Study* (1965), requires "a systematic critical attitude and intellectual discipline acquired only through practice" (p. 1). This critical attitude is what differentiates "banking education" from a pedagogy of liberation. Study is not consuming ideas but re-creating them, Freire remarks. Therefore, to study someone's scholarship supposes "the analysis of the one who through study wrote it" (Freire, 1965, p. 1). It is addressing the *Otro*, reading his/her words, that we study.

Consequently, Pinar adds, "study—not teaching—is the site of education" (Pinar, 2015, p. 11). As a way of life, study "supports subjective and social reconstruction threaded through academic knowledge and everyday life" (Pinar, 2015, p. 11). This suggested connection between popular and erudite knowledge is present in the concept of study. As a process of self-formation then, study seems to have the potential to bridge orality and literacy. One could advance the idea that, through that process, study also becomes a way of conversation, a place for dialogical encounter among oral and written traditions. This is also part of the cosmopolitan resonance of the word study.

Second Constellation: Currere *and* Bildung[6]

> I only became aware of reconceptualization as an element of North American curriculum theory preparing the Oslo-Conference "Didaktik and/or curriculum" (August 1995), thanks to Svefan Hopmann. If I have read William F. Pinar's 1978 essay, "The Reconceptualization of Curriculum Studies, correctly, the reconceptualists' position is similar to critical constructive Didaktik in significant areas.
>
> (Klafki, 1998, p. 327)

Unlike the previous constellation, this second one has been already advanced by an increasing number of works that interest themselves with the connections between these two traditions: Curriculum and *Didaktik* (Autio, 2014, 2009, 2006; Gundem & Hopmann, 1998a; Hopmann & Riquarts, 1995a; Pinar, 2011, 2009; Westbury, Hopmann, & Riquarts, 2000). These writings are also connected with scholars participating in the movement of the internationalization of Curriculum Studies, though not exclusively. Tero Autio (2014, 2006, 2007), for instance, has situated these two important traditions in a broader theoretical and historical framework, namely modernity. To him, both traditions begin around the beginning of the seventeenth century and both are inextricably linked to the phenomenon of schooling. Autio acknowledges, however, Westbury's (2000) insight that these two traditions are "embedded in very different practical, cultural and structural contexts" (pp. 47–78); posing "major problems of intercultural communication" (Gundem & Hopmann, 1998b, p. 1). Nevertheless, to Autio (2014, 2007, 2006), Curriculum Studies and

Didaktik are theories of curriculum with striking commonalities in their instrumental and humanistic venues.

> If the Pinnacle of the regulation of the selves in the American curriculum was a "learner" around whose behavior the empirically produced psychological discourse would legitimize the universal features of the subject and, a different but discursively similar project of control, is manifest in *Didaktik* discourse. "Conformity of wills" was a more convincing form of political and educational discourse among more homogeneous population in the post-1800 as a common history and language, similar geographical locales, and shared contestation between religious and cultural values bind people together. In this context the nation-state as a particular form of organization on the interactions of people became possible and desirable.
> (Autio, 2006, p. 11)

Along similar lines, Hamilton and Gudmundsdottir (1994) in their report on the Kiel Symposium[7] comment:

> Separation of 'What?' questions from 'How?' questions, for instance, haunt discussion of Anglo-Saxon curriculum practice. Equivalent problems also exercise Didaktik theorists. What, for instance, is the relationship between Didaktik and Methodik? In turn, these internal difficulties are compounded if comparable questions are asked about the relationship between Anglo-Saxon conceptions of curriculum and German notions of Didaktik.
> (p. 345)

Like Autio, Hamilton and Gudmundsdottir (1994) also adhere to the idea of commonalities. They emphasize the similar social context in which both traditions originated, namely "modern schooling" (p. 346). Furthermore, the distinctions fade when both traditions face our present circumstances and think about a future for education. Hamilton and Gudmundsdottir (1994) claim that these two traditions, rather than ask themselves what they are, should ask what they should become, and how—maybe "pointing to a historical convergence" (Hamilton, 1995, p. 71). Furthermore, Klafki (1995) sustains that "a comparison of a large number of attempts to define the object of Didaktik (and its research) with corresponding attempts to define the object of curriculum theory (and its research) reveal a large degree of overlap and agreement" (p. 187). According to this, Klafki continues, "it would often be more appropriate to speak of "didaktik/curriculum theory" (p. 188).

Those and other insights formulated more than two decades ago have evolved in the increasing literature on the relations between Curriculum Studies and *Didaktik* alluded to at the beginning of this section, as well as in the increasing scholarship available in English focused on the concept in *Bildung* (Horlacher, 2017, 2012, 2004; Tyson, 2016; Hu, 2015; Bohlin, 2013; Kim, 2013; Schneider, 2012; Siljander, Kivelä, & Sutinen, 2012; Oelkers, 2011; HammershØj, 2009; Hopmann, 2007; Sunker, 2007; Vinterbo-Hohr & Hohr, 2006; Thompson, 2005; Bauer, 2003; Biesta, 2003, 2002; Løvlie, 2002; Løvlie & Standish, 2002; Hamilton, 1998, 1995; Terhart, 1998, 1995; Westbury, 1998, 1995). The description of this field of correspondences concentrates now on the concepts of *currere* and *Bildung*; through these both traditions seem to focus their critique of instrumental reason, as well as the centrality of self-cultivation and knowledge.

Critique of Instrumental Reason

Instrumental reason structures modernity. Modern disciplines include this instrumental aspect. The educational traditions born alongside modernity are not free of it. As theories of schooling, both Curriculum Studies and *Didaktik* have the "propensity for reductionism by universalizing, standardizing and normalizing—and, by the same token, marginalizing and segregating—linguistic, cultural and racial [as well as gender] differences" (Autio, 2009, p. 2). Therefore, Autio continues, these two "curriculum traditions, Curriculum Studies and *Didaktik*, are intellectual heirs of the Enlightenment yet in different ways" (p. 2). "My own hypothesis is that both resonate with the idea of order," Hamilton (1995, p. 78) suggests, answering to the question of intersections between curriculum and *Didaktik* in the beginning of the sixteenth century. Nevertheless, there is also an emancipatory project in modernity coexisting with instrumental reason (Habermas, 1987)—an emancipatory project and sacrificial myth (Dussel, 1995, 1996). Autio suggests that the reconceptualization movement and the reaction to educational standardization are also part of this common heritage. In other words, to address the critique of instrumental reason *Bildung* and curriculum, reconceptualized as *currere*, perform the critique of technocratic modernity.

Currere was a main concept in the critique of curriculum development, psychologized curriculum (Autio, 2006), and Tyler's rationale: "a scientific universalism generated by psychological discourse of a "learner" intertwined with the social requirements to rule-obeying behavior as a citizen" (p. 11). *Currere* reconceptualizes curriculum as the study of educational experience beyond the frames of social engineering, encouraging "theoretical curiosity that create[s] a spring board for more genuine interdisciplinary discourses in the field" (p. 15). *Currere* is lived curriculum, not only what is prescribed. Therefore, "it seems to revive and critically revise hermeneutical interests both within curriculum studies and the Didaktik tradition" (p. 103). Accordingly, curriculum is no longer, or at least not only, the multilevel procedural organization of the shaping of the subject but also an effort to understand life as educational. It is, in Pinar's Sartrean language, the internal experience of the external structures. It is this recontextualization of the educational thinking landscape that makes Autio affirm that Pinar belongs not in the Anglo-Saxon field of curriculum but in the European tradition of *Bildung*, a concept that, according to him, has always had a democratic communicative connotation in Scandinavia (Autio, 2006, 2009). Along these lines, Hopmann and Riquarts (1995a) have affirmed that "[i]t is one of the curious anachronism of the discussion that the picture of German didaktik in the Nordic countries is still coloured by *critical theory* . . ., which facilitates the coupling of didaktik with American versions of *critical* curriculum research" (p. 30). This feature has affected the reception of curriculum discourses in those windy landscapes where the continental tradition of *Bildung* blows.

Bildung has been also used as a concept to resist educational technocratic globalization. Daniel Tröhler (2011), for example, has pointed out that in educational discourses in Europe, the concept of *Bildung* is usually called in opposition to standardization. Regardless of the difficulties of defining *Bildung*, Tröhler (2012) points to Wolff-Metternich (2004), in that there seems to be an agreement about what *Bildung* is not: "*Bildung* . . . is not codifiable and fixable knowledge—neither theoretically nor practically," she stated, "not utilitarian and not pragmatic" (p. 69) and therefore "principally purposeless" (p. 149). This view is rooted in the history of *Bildung* and the arrival of education at the German university, both connected to anti-Western ideology. Therefore, it seems consistent for the concept of *Bildung* to be perceived as fundamental to the German ideal of education among the reaction to international standardized testing, usually understood as part of globalization and thus Americanization.

This critique of instrumental reason was also made by one of the main figures of the Frankfurt School, Theodor Adorno, in relation to education. In his critique Adorno uses the main German educational concept *Bildung*, articulating his criticism in his *Theorie der Halbbildung* (1959) or theory of *half-bildung*. According to Adorno, *Bildung* was made into a commodity. It has become *Halbbildung*. Its inherent meanings had been separated from the contingency of human affairs. *Bildung* has become a commodity the possession of which provides exchange value. *Bildung* was used by the bourgeoisie to emancipate itself but that *use value* was not passed on to the lower classes. *Halbbildung* is *Bildung* without its use value. In Adorno's terms, the "dehumanization brought about by the capitalist mode of production denied the workers everything necessary for culture, beginning with leisure" (p. 7). Leisure is a requirement for an education that wants to remain education and not just half education. It is interesting how Adorno connects the idea of a true *Bildung* to leisure, as a requirement for human education. What remains in an education without leisure becomes rushed, precluding contemplation and tending toward training. Pieper, also a German author, uses the word *Bildung* only once in his *Leisure: The Basis of Culture* (1963), when he distinguishes true education (*Bildung*) from mere training. Is it really only leisure that can provide the basis for true *Bildung*? Is it only when the use value of cultural goods prevails over their exchange value? The answer seems to be yes.

According to Adorno (1959), experience has been replaced by the "selective, disconnected, interchangeable and ephemeral state of being informed which, as one can already observe, will promptly be cancelled by other information" (p. 33). Therefore, it is impossible to establish tradition within the individual, because the continuity of external experience has been broken. *Halbbildung* shields people from experience, turning subjects of learning into objects of consumption. Adorno accepts a certain emancipatory potential in *Bildung* as an ideal linked to autonomy, emancipation, and humanity. Stojanov (2013), drawing on Adorno, points out that *Bildung* is both the adjustment to and inclusion into a given society and the opening of one's eyes to an objective world, cultivating the ability to reflect critically on it. In order for *Bildung* to remain *Bildung*, it needs *Erziehung* as an "emancipatory pedagogical action" (Stojanov, 2013, p. 8). I think that this conception of *Bildung* is close to Habermas's intellectual endeavor of reading modernity as an incomplete project. Actually, Adorno's search for the missing half of *Bildung* in *Erziehung*[8] is similar to Habermas's search in the life-world.

What must be done is a deep social-psychoanalysis in order to understand the actual crisis in *Bildung*, as well as an education that combines *Bildung* and *Erziehung*. This education is a condition for the development of progressive consciousness without which education becomes mis-education. After Auschwitz, the only education that has any sense "is an education toward critical self-reflection" (Adorno, 1967, p. 20). Through such education, the developing of progressive consciousness can be reached. This progressive consciousness is a condition for autonomy.

Self-Formation

Self-formation is a constitutive element of the concept of *Bildung*, or *Selbsbildung* (Klafki, 2000). In the German *Bildung/Didaktik* tradition, Autio (2009) has pointed out, "Bildung can be understood as a kind of self-formation along the lines of a wider belonging and where Didaktik refers generally to the pedagogical techniques for intertwining if not spiraling subjectivity and society together" (p. 11). Self-cultivation or self-formation is the dimension of *Bildung* increasingly highlighted in English translations of that German word. The resonances with Pinar's concept of *currere* are evident in this and they have been made explicit in his work *The Character of Curriculum Studies: Currere, Bildung, and the Recurrent Question of the Subject* (2011). There, Pinar addresses the question by claiming that the subject, as an individual and as subject matter, has been central to Curriculum Studies in the United States. Historically situated, this discussion connects to a main concern of American culture: the individual. The individual is an imagined subject whom schooling helps to shape, but it is also a flesh and body person who experiences that process. The problem of the individual, the person, the subject, in Curriculum Studies is put into perspective through the concept of *currere* as lived curriculum, as one's educational experience and through the German concept of *Bildung* as self-cultivation. Both concepts are central in thinking about the relation between culture and subject, and, how is it defined historically and lived biographically. Neither in *currere* nor in *Bildung* does education occur in isolation. The cultivation of one's personal uniqueness is already social, therefore political, since it requires communication with others, a dialogical encounter.

In the interplay of the planned curriculum and the lived curriculum (Aoki, 2005; Furlán, 1981) opens a "Zone in Between" (Aoki, 2005) in which the conversation about our educational experience becomes complicated, and that complicated conversation with "layered voices" "uncannily correct" and "elusively true" (p. 187) is what Curriculum Studies is all about. That is why

> the concept of *currere* forefronts the meaning of the curriculum as complicated conversation encouraging educational experience. Indeed, *currere* emphasizes the everyday experience of the individual and his or her capacity to learn from that experience, to reconstruct experience through thought and dialogue to enable understanding.
> (Pinar, 2011, p. 2)

The focus on the personal and experiential led Pinar to ground *currere* in phenomenology, existentialism, and psychoanalysis (Pinar & Grumet, 1976; Pinar et al., 1995; Kincheloe, 1998). As he claims, "*currere* historically rooted in the field of curriculum is existentialism, phenomenology, and psychoanalysis, in the study of educational experience" (Pinar, 1975, p. 400). The traditions called upon are concerned with the relation between the social and the personal and that concern underlies *currere* as a process of self-study.

Therefore, such a process of self-knowledge is never complete and always retrospective. *Currere*, as the autobiographical *regressive-progressive-analytic-synthetic* method to study the lived curriculum, can be useful in this reconstruction. As a process of ongoing reconstruction, subjective and social, self-knowledge entails becoming subjective by becoming historical; and in becoming a subject, the canonical curriculum question—*what knowledge is of most worth?*—recurs, Pinar (2011) insists. Therefore, the centrality of academic knowledge in self-formation is emphasized.

> Expressing one's individuality through subject matter—the public discussion of one's private thoughts—cannot be sidestepped if the subjective complexity and coherence required by democracy are to

be cultivated. *Bildung*—"the self-reflexive cultivation of character" (Anderson, 2006, p. 48)—has taught us the significance of spirituality in self-formation, its cosmopolitan capacity to open us to difference, and the inestimable importance of those with whom we share the historical moment and its emplacement.

(Pinar, 2012, p. 143)

Knowledge

Discussing the relation between Curriculum Studies and *Didaktik*, Hopmann and Riquarts (1995a) see the importance of content as a possible contribution of this German tradition to the Anglo-Saxon field of curriculum. In the tradition of *Bildung*-centered *Didaktik* (Deng, 2015; Vásquez-Levy, 2002), the concept of *Bildung* is also related to knowledge as cultural content, as knowledge of the world. W. Von Humboldt, in the context of the German enlightenment, was the one who formulated the concept of *Bildung* and its practice in the development of the Prussian school system and the foundation of the University of Berlin. In his celebrated "Excerpt," Humboldt (1793) defined the ideal of *Bildung* as "the highest and most harmonious development of his [human] powers to a complete and consistent whole" (p. 58). This is possible "by connecting our self with the world and thereby creating the most general, most active and free interaction," Humboldt continues (p. 58). This Humboldtian definition of *Bildung* includes the "belief in the possibility of moral education through knowledge" (p. 166), an important reminder since the debates about the concept of *Bildung* overlap in the nineteenth century with the problems of what content or school subjects should be part of the curriculum in the *Gymnasium*. In other words, the concept of *Bildung* is historically connected to the problematic of what knowledge is of most worth, the canonical question in Curriculum Studies (Pinar, 2012; Apple, 2010[9]); a "classical curriculum analogue of Didaktik analysis," Hamilton (1998, p. 80) reminds us, referring to Spencer's question "What knowledge is of most worth?" It was the time in which general education was being discussed, which made the school subjects of the gymnasium even more important, since it is the institutional passage to the university. Usually associated with the humanities, the concept of *Bildung* was facing tendencies that saw the natural sciences as desirable to be taught at the German *Gymnasium*. For instance,

> Herder criticized the school, which in his opinion was obsolete and frozen, and he demanded reform that would teach the students "living" knowledge, meaning that school instruction should focus more on school subjects that deal with "real" things, such as mathematics and biology (as opposed to languages).
>
> (Horlacher, 2012, p. 139)

In a more contemporary context, Klafki's reformulation of the concept of *Bildung*, informed by Habermas's communicative action, preserves this potential for contributing to educational decisions. To him, in talking about *Didaktik* and/or curriculum "the element in question is content" (Klafki, 1995, p. 187); therefore, the word *critical* in *critical-constructive Didaktik* "applies to an interest in knowledge" (p. 191). What is at stake is a "pedagogy of substance" (Shulman, 1995) in which one finds remarkable resonances between a pedagogical conception on two sides of the Atlantic. In this sense, "categorical *Bildung* guides the selection of learning contents according to the principles of the elementary, fundamental, and exemplary" (Horlacher, 2012, p. 142). This potential of *Bildung* as guiding educational decisions concerning the content of schooling is certainly related with Humboldt's conceptualization as "connecting our self with the world," namely the objectivities of the world in bodies of knowledge that may or not become subject matters. Along these lines, Stojanov (2012) points out:

> *Bildung* presupposes a sense of objectivity and attitude of taking objects as having unique forms and intrinsic values as well as immanent meanings in themselves. Without this objective pole of the world, which requires an intellectual effort to apprehend, the overcoming of the subjective dimension of the educational process is impossible.
> (p. 128)

In other words, the subject matters act as the "non-I" that the "I" requires in order to self-form himself or herself. Hence, "increasing one's personal knowledge—the acquisition of the outside world, or world 'without'—therefore has a significantly deeper importance than multiplying one's store of information" (Horlacher, 2012, p. 139). That is very close to Pinar's formulation of self-cultivation through academic study. The question for the subject of educational experience is also the question for the subject matter. "Our calling [he declares] is not to cram but to encourage children to explore their subjective singularity, their historical subjecthood, through subject matter" (Pinar, 2011, p. 143). This is maybe most clearly expressed in Pinar's attempt to reconceptualize curriculum development through the production of synoptic texts.

These synoptic texts juxtapose the two structures (intellectual history and present circumstances) in order to *synthetize* an area of scholarship relevant to the complicated conversation that curriculum is. These works[10] take the form of montages that create images of "especially interdisciplinary configurations not visible in the compartmentalized curriculum organized around school subjects and focused on standardized exams" (Pinar, 2006, p. 5). In this sense, it is possible to intuit a connection between the definition of curriculum as conversation and curriculum as a field of study. These texts seek to be a place for a dialogical encounter among teachers and students.

Curriculum Studies as a Force Field

The word curriculum[11] is the first word in the title of this book, *Curriculum Studies as an International Conversation*. I have addressed in Chapter 2 the "content" words I am using to name my work. My search is dialogical—through words. Those words, I have argued, act as centers of force fields of meaning in which different traditions are brought together forming a constellation. Words, then, act like force fields around which intellectual traditions gravitate. It is now time to address the force field of curriculum.

The idea of tensions within the field is evident in the reflection of the scholars that cultivate it. William Schubert (2010), for example, has pointed out that there is a historical "tension between the expansion of curriculum ideas and the need to summarize them for dissemination" (p. 18). I wonder whether it is possible to find some "common cause and common understanding across our vast landscape of difference" (Hlebowitsh, 2010, p. 15) in today's moment, which seems unequivocally dominated by the expansion of divergent intellectual projects that move in different directions. I believe, though, that is not just the weakness but also the strength of the field "that (supposedly) is there to help us think rigorously about what and whose knowledge is of most worth" (Apple, 2010, p. 100).[12]

In the midst of such a divergence, the only thing holding the field together seems to be the word that names the field: Curriculum, a word that alludes to a certain hybrid vocation that Curriculum Studies is addressing as an international conversation. In fact, although Anglo-Saxon, this tradition is named using the Latin word "curriculum," usually translated as a course of study. This *technical term* was first used as such in the United Kingdom, specifically in Glasgow in 1643, as has been pointed out by David Hamilton (1989) in his classic work *On the Origins of the Educational Terms Class and Curriculum*. He writes:

> To this extent, 'curriculum' seems to have confirmed the idea—already reflected in the adoption of 'class'—that the different elements of an educational course were to be treated as all-of-a-piece. Any course worthy of the name was to embody both 'disciplina' (a sense of structural coherence), and 'ordo' (a sense of internal sequencing). Thus, to speak of a post-Reformation 'curriculum' is to point to an educational entity that exhibits both structural wholeness and sequential completeness. A 'curriculum' should not only be 'followed'; it should also be 'completed'. Whereas the sequence, length and completeness of medieval courses had been relatively open to student negotiation (for example, at Bologna) and/or teacher abuse (for example, in Paris), the emergence of 'curriculum' brought, I suggest, a greater sense of control to both teaching and learning.
>
> (Hamilton, 2009, p. 11)

Hamilton's etymological curiosity,[13] as Freire would call it, left us a legacy of informative and suggestive texts about the connections between the words curriculum, school class, discipline, and order in the initial centuries of modernity. It should be noticed also that the historical context of Reform and Counter-reform shaped the initial configuration of modern schooling, not a context very open to embrace hybridity; and also a definitely "oxymoronic" context, if we do not forget what was happening in the underside of modernity.

From Polysemy to Analogy

In addition to its hybrid appeal, the word curriculum has a distinctive trait that makes it suitable to the work of building an international intellectual field informed by intercultural dialogue in which claims of absolute incompatibilities and impossible communication can turn into relative commonalities and possible bridging dialogues. This characteristic is its polysemy.[14]

Polysemy has certainly been regarded as a negative trait that leads to equivocation. However, what would happen if we think of the word "curriculum" as analogical? Then its capacity to incorporate different meanings might become its strength rather than its weakness. This is to say, an analogical understanding of the word curriculum enables intercultural dialogue across educational traditions. It suggests that there is no unsurpassable difference but analogies, "a possible convergence" (Hamilton, 1998, p. 79) that a work of elective affinities helps to recognize, while both subjects in the dialogue are honored for their distinctiveness. This analogical understanding is a gain that comes from the initial approach of the *analéctica latinoamericana* and the concept of elective affinities. I believe there is in the study of the resonances of both traditions a methodological potential that might contribute to the development of a cosmopolitan scholarship in Curriculum Studies.

Nevertheless, since that cosmopolitan scholarship entails dialogical encounters inside and outside of the tradition of Curriculum Studies, one could ask why keep the word curriculum to name a worldwide field of education. It is a fair question, considering that different traditions name differently their efforts to study schooling. Tero Autio (2006), who situates his work "between and beyond" the two main Western educational traditions, has advanced the idea of different curriculum theories. This move seems to acknowledge that even when one may want to go beyond, we are already in the middle. In fact, as I have tried to show, the word "curriculum" has already made its way to other educational traditions as an "American" import, becoming part of the search of various intellectual communities in Europe, Africa, Asia, Oceania, and *Latinoamérica*. Even the recent educational reform in China is taking the tradition of curriculum to a cultural geography beyond what can be called "the west." Autio (2009) writes

> China's modernization may signal a cultural feedback to western notions of modernity and a future of the emergence of contested modernities. If we think of the enlightenment as a great educational project, China's modernization, and its global cultural impact would imply the urge for reconsideration of the European Bildung/Didaktik as well as Anglo-American curriculum as two master narratives of curriculum theory.
>
> (p. 20)

Taking all this into consideration, it seems that the intellectual field of curriculum is reaching true global dimensions. Working through the past is an ethical-epistemological requirement for each tradition willing to address intercultural dialogue within and without.

Notes

1. In Chile, as in many Latin American countries, to earn a Bachelor's degree one is usually required to write a thesis. This requirement has a high exigency in fields such as those in the humanities and social sciences.
2. This historical periodification was used in the first chapter to address "internationalization" as a dimension of Curriculum Studies.
3. In the United States, the crisis of the Sputnik and the educational reform in the 1960s, among other factors, co-helped to provoke a main gap in the field: the gap between curriculum development and Curriculum Theory. The latter was no longer concerned with the development of curriculum prescription, but with understanding curriculum as lived educational experience. Kridel (2010) has argued that Curriculum Studies "designates a shift of theory and practice as scholars sought understanding of curricula as a phenomena of interest and societal import in contrast with sole concentration on service to leaders of practice in schools" (p. 230). As a result, the field of Curriculum Studies has been fractured, broadly speaking, among those working in curriculum design and those doing Curriculum Theory. Therefore, this complicated field has been incapable of, and reluctant to, offering a unified view of the field (Johnson-Mardones, 2015, p. 2).
4. The term is taken by Pinar (2004, 2012) from the following quote: "[T]he post-Sputnik educational atmosphere has quickened the activities of those who demand more educational rigor, who can now argue that we are engaged in mortal educational combat with the Soviet Union" (Hofstadter, 1962, p. 358).
5. Pinar is referring here to the very well-known diagnosis of curriculum as "moribund" made by Schwab in his *The Practical: The Language of Curriculum* (1969), and others characterizations regarding the field as arrested, dying, and so on that Huebner, Pinar, and others used during that period.
6. What is *Bildung*? *Bildung* is the central concept of German thought on education. It is one of the "fundamental principles" in German pedagogy (Horlacher, 2012). Etymologically, it means to shape according to an image, to acquire a form. Historically, it is connected to the Catholic concept of *Bildunga*, having

a mystic connotation. German idealism brought the concept into philosophy during the seventeenth century. However, the inclusion and development of *Bildung* as an educational concept occurred during the late eighteenth century, in the context of the *Aufklärung* (Enlightenment). Ever since, *Bildung* has been a central part of every discourse on education in Germany, having also a strong influence in central Europe and Scandinavia. This centrality, however, does not make the concept less elusive. It has been pointed out that *Bildung* is a container word, a word that can convey a variety of meanings. Moreover, Dohmen (1964) has claimed that *Bildung* is one of the most ambiguous and vague fundamental concepts of German educational thought.

7. The Kiel Symposium took place at the Institute for Science Education, Christian-Albretchs-Universität in 1993. The symposium marked a turn from the "and/or" to the concern for the common roots of *Curriculum* and *Didaktik*.
8. Gundem & Hopmann (1998b) refine *Erziehung* as "formation by external influences like parents and teachers." (p. 2)
9. Without renouncing his opposing question "whose knowledge?", Apple has paired together both question in a piece on Huebner published in Curriculum Inquiry, affirming that Curriculum Studies' purpose is to help us to think "what and whose knowledge is of most worth" (Apple, 2010, p. 100).
10. See, for example, Pinar (2008, 2007, and 2006).
11. "The first thing to observe in a global scales is that the concept of curriculum is not equally central everywhere. In France, is a term only recently imported into the French language (Egéa-Kuehne, 2003), and pedagogy has long been a more important concern than the course of study.... Meanwhile, didactics (Didaktik in German) is a key word in Germany and Russia ... and it has become important in the past two decades in France as well" (Anderson-Levit, 2008, p. 351).
12. These centrifugal tendencies "are certainly a consequence of the field's history during the last decades of the twentieth century. This history is marked by the reconceptualization of curriculum studies in the United States and the incorporation of phenomenology, existentialism, psychoanalysis, critical theory, biography, gender, race, and class analysis, postmodernism, poststructuralism, and so on, in the project of understanding curriculum" (Johnson-Mardones, 2014, p. 3).
13. Hamilton (2009) explains: "My historical inquiries grew from my experiences as a schoolteacher in the 1960s. Throughout, I have been steered by etymological curiosity. When, for instance, had key words—like class and curriculum—first appeared? In my case, however, I had little historical knowledge or training. This greatly affected how I worked. My original purpose was to write something that would help educationists understand their place in history. My inquiries were—and still are—motivated by the aphorism 'Once you know what you are doing, you are no longer doing it.'"
14. "The polysemy of the word has been traditionally pointed out by listing the multiple definitions that the authors in the field have offered over time. These definitions have been organized, for instance, by distinguishing between those that can be labelled as prescriptive and those that can be termed descriptive. In the field of curriculum, prescription abounds while descriptions are scarce, Stenhouse affirmed in England, beginning in the 1970s. The same criticism was taking place in the United States from the late 1970s for those concerned with a field dominated by the so-called Tyler rationale [Kliebard, 1977]. Since then, Jackson [1968] named a hidden curriculum taking place in schools, Schwab called for the practical as the language of curriculum, and the next decade brought a vibrant scholarship seeking to reconceptualize the

field. All that brought up a proliferation of new definitions. Those definitions were put into classifications and typologies, which proliferated just as the definitions did" (Johnson-Mardones, 2014, p. 4).

References

Adorno, T. W. (1967/2003). Education after Auschwitz. In R. Tiedemann (Ed.). *Can one live after Auschwitz? A philosophical reader* (pp. 19–36). Stanford, CA: Stanford University Press.

Adorno, T. W. (1959/1980). Theorie der Halbbildung. In *Gesammelte Schriften* (Vol. 8, pp. 93–121). Frankfurt: Suhrkamp.

Anderson-Levit, K. (2008). Globalization and curriculum. In M. Connelly, M. F. He, & J. Phillion (Eds.). *The Sage handbook of curriculum and instruction* (pp. 349–368). Los Angeles, CA: Sage Publications.

Aoki, T. (2005). *Curriculum in a new key: The collected works of Ted Aoki*. Mahwah, NJ: Lawrence Erlbaum Associates.

Apple, M. W. (2010). Fly and the fly bottle: On Dwayne Huebner, the uses of language, and the nature of the curriculum field. *Curriculum Inquiry, 40*(1), 95–103.

Autio, T. (2014). The internationalization of curriculum research. In W. F. Pinar (Ed.). *International handbook of curriculum research* (2nd ed., pp. 17–31). Mahwah, NJ: Lawrence Erlbaum Associates.

Autio, T. (2009). Globalization, curriculum, and new belongings of subjectivity. In E. Ropo & T. Autio (Eds.). *International conversations on curriculum studies: Subject, society and curriculum* (pp. 1–22). Rotterdam: Sense Publishers.

Autio, T. (2007). Towards European curriculum studies: Reconsidering some basic tenets of Bildung and Didaktik. *Journal of the American Association for the Advancement of Curriculum Studies, 3*(1), 1–11.

Autio, T. (2006). *Subjectivity, curriculum and society: Between and beyond German Didaktik and Anglo-American curriculum studies*. Mahwah, NJ: Lawrence Erlbaum Associates.

Bauer, W. (2003). On the relevance of Bildung for democracy. *Educational Philosophy and Theory, 35*(2), 211–225.

Biesta, G. (2003). How general can bildung be? Reflections on the future of a modern educational ideal. *Journal of Philosophy of Education, 36*(3), 377–390.

Biesta, G. (2002). Bildung and modernity: The future of Bildung in a world of difference. *Studies in Philosophy and Education, 21*, 343–351.

Block, A. (2004). *Talmud, curriculum, and the practical: Joseph Schwab and the Rabbis*. New York, NY: Peter Lang.

Bobbitt, F. (1918). *The curriculum*. Boston: Houghton Mifflin.

Bohlin, H. (2013). Bildung and intercultural understanding. *Intercultural Education, 24*(5), 391–400.

Bruner, J. (1983). *In search of mind: Essays in autobiography*. New York, NY: Harper & Row.

Camilloni, A. (2007). *El saber didáctico*. Buenos Aires: Paidos.

Deng, Z. (2015). Content, Joseph Schwab and German Didaktik. *Journal of Curriculum Studies, 47*(6), 773–786.

Dewey, J. (1902). *The child and the curriculum*. Chicago, IL: University of Chicago Press.

Dohmen, G. (1964). *Bildung und Schule Die Entstehung des deutschen Bildungsbegriffs und die Entwicklung seines Verhältnisses zur Schule Bd 1: Der religiöse und der organologische Bildungsbegriff.* Weinheim: Beltz.
Dussel, E. (2013). *Ethics of liberation in the age of globalization and exclusion.* Durham: Duke University Press.
Dussel, E. (2011). *Politics of liberation: A critical world history.* London: SCM Press.
Dussel, E. (1996). *The underside of modernity: Apel, Ricoeur, Rorty, Taylor, and the philosophy of liberation.* Atlantic Highlands, NY: Humanities Press.
Dussel, E. (1995). *The invention of the Americas: Eclipse of "the other" and the myth of modernity.* New York, NY: Continuum.
Dussel, E. (1985). *Philosophy of liberation.* New York, NY: Orbis Books.
Dussel, E. (1980). *La pedagógica latinoamericana.* Bogotá: Editorial Nueva América.
Dussel, E. (1974). Domination-liberation: A new approach. *Concilium*, 96(1), 34–56.
Dussel, E. (1973a). *Para una ética de la liberación latinoamericana.* Buenos Aires: Siglo Veintiuno Argentina Editores. V1.
Dussel, E. (1973b). *Para una ética de la liberación latinoamericana.* Buenos Aires: Siglo Veintiuno Argentina Editores. V2.
Egéa-Kuehne, D. (2003). Understanding curriculum in France: A multifaceted approach to thinking education. In W. F. Pinar (Ed.). *Handbook of research on curriculum* (1st ed., pp. 329–366). Mahwah, NJ: Lawrence Erlbaum Associates.
Furlán, A. (1981). *El curriculum pensado y el curriculum vivido.* Paper presented in the V Jornadas sobre problemas de enseñanza-aprendizaje en el área de la salud. ENEP-Tztacala, UNAM, Mexico.
Freire, P. (1970/2000). *Pedagogy of the oppressed.* New York, NY: Continuum.
Freire, P. (1965). The act of study. In P. Freire (1985). *The politics of education* (pp. 1–6). Westport, CN: Bergin & Garvey Publishers.
Freire, P., & Shor, I. (1987). *A pedagogy for liberation: Dialogues on transforming.* South Hadley, MA: Bergin & Garvey Publishers.
Gilloch, G., (2002). *Walter Benjamin: Critical constellations.* Cambridge, UK: Polity.
Gundem, B., & Hopmann, S. (Eds.) (1998a). *Didaktik and/or curriculum: An international dialogue.* New York, NY: Peter Lang.
Gundem, B., & Hopmann, S. (1998b). Introduction: Didaktik meets curriculum. In B. Gundem & S. Hopmann (Eds.) (1998). *Didaktik and/or curriculum: An international dialogue* (pp. 1–8). New York, NY: Peter Lang.
Habermas, J. (1987). *The philosophical discourse of modernity: Twelve lectures.* Cambridge, MA: MIT Press.
Hamilton, D. (2009). On the origins of the educational terms class and curriculum. In B. Baker (Ed.). *New curriculum history* (pp. 3–20). Rotterdam: Sense Publishers.
Hamilton, D. (1998). Didaktik, deliberation and reflection (In search of the common places). In B. Gundem & S. Hopmann (Eds.) (1998). *Didaktik and/or curriculum: An international dialogue* (pp. 79–86). New York, NY: Peter Lang.
Hamilton, D. (1995). Order and structure in Didaktik and curriculum. In S. Hopmann & K. Riquarts (Eds.). *Didaktik and/or curriculum* (pp. 71–84). Kiel: Institut für die Pädagogik der Naturwissenschaften.

Hamilton, D. (1989). *Toward a theory of schooling*. London: Falmer Press.
Hamilton, D., & Gudmundsdottir, S. (1994). Didaktic and/or Curriculum? *Pedagogy, Culture & Society*, 2(3), 345–350.
HammershØj, L. G. (2009). Creativity as a question of bildung. *Journal of Philosophy of Education*, 43(4), 545–558.
Hlebowitsh, P. (2010). Centripetal thinking in curriculum studies. *Curriculum Inquiry*, 40(4), 503–513.
Hofstadter, R. (1962). *Antiintellectualism in American life*. New York, NY: Knop.
Hopmann, S. T. (2007). Restrained teaching: The common core of Didaktik. *European Educational Research Journal*, 6(2), 109–124.
Hopmann, S., & Riquarts, K. (1995a). Didaktik and/or curriculum: Basic problems of comparative Didaktik. In S. Hopmann & K. Riquarts (Eds.). *Didaktik and/or curriculum* (pp. 9–40). Kiel: Institut für die Pädagogik der Naturwissenschaften.
Hopmann, S., & Riquarts, K. (Eds.) (1995b). *Didaktik and/or curriculum*. Kiel: Institut für die Pädagogik der Naturwissenschaften.
Horlacher, R. (2017). *The educated subject and the German concept of Bildung: A comparative cultural history*. New York, NY: Routledge.
Horlacher, R. (2012). What is Bildung? or: Why cannot we get away from the concept of bildung? In P. Siljander, Pauli., A. Kivelä & A. Sutinen (Eds.). *Theories of Bildung and growth: Connections and controversies between continental educational thinking and American pragmatism* (pp. 135–147). Rotterdam: Sense Publishers.
Horlacher, R. (2004). Bildung: A construction of a history of philosophy of education. *Studies in Philosophy and Education*, 23(1), 409–426.
Hu, A. (2015). The idea of Bildung in the current educational discourse. *L2 Journal*, 7(4), 17–19.
Humboldt, W. (1793). Theory of Bildung. In I. Westbury, S. Hopmann, & K. Riquarts (Eds.) (2000). *Teaching as a reflective practice: The German Didaktik tradition* (pp. 57–62). Mahwah, NJ: Erlbaum.
Jackson, P. W. (Ed.) (1992). *Handbook of research on curriculum: A project of the American Educational Research Association*. New York. NY: Macmillan.
Jackson, P. W. (1968). *Life in classrooms*. New York, NY: Holt, Rinehart and Winston.
Johnson-Mardones, D. (2015). Understating curriculum as phenomenon, field and design: A multidimensional conceptualization. *Journal of International Dialogues in Education*, 2(2), 1–9.
Johnson-Mardones, D. (2014). Toward a multidimensional concept of curriculum. *European Journal of Curriculum Studies*, 1(2), 72–77.
Kim, J. H. (2013). Teacher action research as Bildung: An application of Gadamer's philosophical hermeneutics to teacher professional development. *Journal of Curriculum Studies*, 45(3), 379–393.
Kincheloe, J. (1998). Pinar's currere and identity in hiperreality: Grounding the post-formal notion of intrapersonal intelligence. In W. Pinar (Ed.). *Curriculum: Toward new identities* (pp. 129–142). New York, NY: Garland.
Klafki, W. (2000). The significance of classical theories of Bildung for a contemporary concept of Allgemeinbildung. In I. Westbury, S. Hopmann, & K. Riquarts (Eds.). *Teaching as a reflective practice: The German Didaktik tradition* (pp. 85–107). Mahwah, NJ: Erlbaum.

Klafki, W. (1998). Characteristics of critical-constructive didaktik. In B. Gundem & S. Hopmann (Eds.) (1998). *Didaktik and/or curriculum: An international dialogue* (pp. 307–330). New York, NY: Peter Lang.

Klafki, W. (1995). On the problem of teaching and learning contents from the stand point of critical-constructive didaktik. In S. Hopmann & K. Riquarts (Eds.). *Didaktik and/or curriculum* (pp. 187–200). Kiel: Institut für die Pädagogik der Naturwissenschaften.

Kliebard, H. M. (1977). The Tyler rationale. In H. Kliebard & A. M. Bellack, (Eds.). *Curriculum and evaluation*. Berkeley, CA: McCutchan.

Kridel, C. (2010). *Encyclopedia of curriculum studies encyclopedia of curriculum studies*. Thousand Oaks, CA: Sage Publications.

Løvlie, L. (2002). The promise of Bildung. *Journal of Philosophy of Education*, 36(3), 467–486.

Løvlie, L., & Standish, P. (2002). Introduction: Bildung and the idea of a liberal education. *Journal of Philosophy of Education*, 36(3), 317–340.

Löwy, M. (1992). *Redemption and utopia: Jewish libertarian thought in Central Europe: A study in elective affinity*. London: Athlone Press.

McCarthy, C. (1990). *Race and curriculum: Social inequality and the theories and politics of difference in contemporary research on schooling*. London: Falmer.

Oelkers, J. (2011). The German concept of "Bildung" then and now. *Lecture at the European college of liberal arts, 1809(December)*, 1–21. Retrieved from www.paed-work.uzh.ch/user_downloads/309/LectureBerlindefdef.pdf

Pieper, J. (1963). *Leisure: The basis of culture*. New York, NY: The New American Library.

Pinar, W. F. (2015). *Educational experience as lived: Knowledge, history, alterity*. New York, NY: Palgrave Macmillan.

Pinar, W. F. (2014). Curriculum research in the United States: Crisis, reconceptualization, internationalization. In W. F. Pinar (Ed.). *International handbook of curriculum research* (2nd ed., pp. 521–532). Mahwah, NJ: Lawrence Erlbaum Associates.

Pinar, W. F. (2013). *Curriculum studies in the United States: Present circumstances, intellectual histories*. Houndmills, NH: Palgrave Macmillan.

Pinar, W. F. (2012). *What is curriculum theory?* New York, NY: Routledge.

Pinar, W. F. (2011). *The character of curriculum studies: Bildung, currere, and the recurring question of the subject*. New York, NY: Palgrave Macmillan.

Pinar, W. F. (2009). Bildung and the internationalization of curriculum studies. In E. Ropo & T. Autio (Eds.). *International conversations on curriculum studies: Subject, society and curriculum* (pp. 1–22). Rotterdam: Sense Publishers.

Pinar, W. F. (2008). Curriculum theory since 1950: Crisis, reconceptualization, internationalization. In M. Connelly, M. F. He, & J. Phillion (Eds.). *The Sage handbook of curriculum and instruction* (pp. 491–513). Los Angeles, CA: Sage Publications.

Pinar, W. F. (2007). *Intellectual advancement through disciplinarity: Verticality and horizontality in curriculum studies*. Rotterdam: Sense Publishers.

Pinar, W. F. (2006). *The synoptic text today and other essays: Curriculum development after the reconceptualization*. New York, NY: Peter Lang.

Pinar, W. F. (2004). *What is curriculum theory?* Mahwah, NJ: Lawrence Erlbaum Associates.

Pinar, W. F., & Grumet, M. (1976). *Toward a poor curriculum*. Dubuque, IA: Kendall/Hunt.

Pinar, W. F. (Ed.) (1975). *Curriculum theorizing: The reconceptualization*. Troy, NY: Educator's International Press.

Pinar, W. F., Reynolds, W. M., Slattery, P., & Taubman, P. M. (1998). Understanding curriculum: A postscript for the next generation. In B. Gundem & S. Hopmann (Eds.) (1998). *Didaktik and/or curriculum: An international dialogue* (pp. 265–306). New York, NY: Peter Lang.

Pinar, W. F., Reynolds, W. M., Slattery, P., & Taubman, P. M. (Eds.) (1995). *Understanding curriculum: An introduction to the study of historical and contemporary curriculum discourses*. New York, NY: Peter Lang.

Schneider, K. (2012). The subject-object transformations and "Bildung". *Educational Philosophy and Theory*, 44(3), 302–311.

Schubert, W. H. (2010). Journeys of expansion and synopsis: Tensions in books that shaped curriculum inquiry, 1968-Present. *Curriculum Inquiry*, 40(1), 17–94.

Schwab, J. (1969). *The practical: A language for curriculum*. Washington, DC: National Education Association.

Shulman, L. (1995). Wisdom for practice and wisdom from practice: To practice of a didactics of substance. In S. Hopmann & K. Riquarts (Eds.). *Didaktik and/or curriculum* (pp. 201–205). Kiel: Institut für die Pädagogik der Naturwissenschaften.

Siljander, P., Kivelä, A., & Sutinen, A. (Eds.) (2012). *Theories of Bildung and growth: Connections and controversies between continental educational thinking and American pragmatism*. Rotterdam: Sense Publishers.

Stojanov, K. (2013). *Education as social critique: On Theodor Adorno's philosophy of education*. Paper presented in the Philosophy of Education Society of Great Britain, Annual Conference, March 22-24, 2013, New College, Oxford.

Stojanov, K. (2012). Theodor w. Adorno—education as social critique. In P. Siljander, A. Kivelä, & A. Sutinen (Eds.). *Theories of Bildung and growth: Connections and controversies between continental educational thinking and American pragmatism* (pp. 125–134). Rotterdam: Sense Publishers.

Sunker, H. (2007). *Politics, Bildung and social justice*. Rotterdam: Sense Publishers.

Terhart, E. (1998). Changing concepts of curriculum: From "Bildung" to "Learning" to "Experience" developments in Germany from de 1960s to 1990. In B. Gundem & S. Hopmann (Eds.) (1998). *Didaktik and/or curriculum: An international dialogue* (pp. 107–126). New York, NY: Peter Lang.

Terhart, E. (1995). Didaktik/curriculum in teacher education: Some German complications. In S. Hopmann & K. Riquarts (Eds.). *Didaktik and/or curriculum* (pp. 187–200). Kiel: Institut für die Pädagogik der Naturwissenschaften.

Thompson, C. (2005). The non-transparency of the self and the ethical value of Bildung. *Journal of Philosophy of Education*, 39(3), 519–533.

Tröhler, D. (2012). The German idea of Bildung and the anti-western ideology. In P. Pauli Siljander, A. Kivelä, & A. Sutinen (Eds.). *Theories of Bildung and growth: Connections and controversies between continental educational thinking and American pragmatism* (pp. 149–164). Rotterdam: Sense Publishers.

Tröhler, D. (2011). *Languages of education: Protestant legacies, national identities, and global aspirations*. New York, NY: Routledge.

Trueit, D. (Ed.) (2003). *The internationalization of curriculum studies: Selected proceedings from the LSU conference 2000*. New York, NY: Peter Lang.

Tyler, R. W. (1949). *Basic principles of curriculum and instruction*. Chicago, IL: University of Chicago Press.
Tyson, R. (2016). What would Humboldt say : A case of general Bildung in vocational education ? *International Journal for Research in Vocational Education and Training*, 3(3), 230–249.
Vásquez-Levy, D. (2002). *Bildung*-centred *Didaktik*: A framework for examining the educational potential of subject matter. *Journal of Curriculum Studies*, 34(1), 117–128.
Vinterbo-Hohr, A., & Hohr, H. (2006). The neo-humanistic concept of Bildung going astray: Comments to Friedrich Schiller's thoughts on education. *Educational Philosophy and Theory*, 38(2), 215–230.
Westbury, I. (2000). Teaching as a reflective practice: What might didaktik teach curriculum. In I. Westbury, S. Hopmann, & K. Riquarts (Eds.) *Teaching as a reflective practice: The German Didaktik tradition* (pp. 15–40). Mahwah, NJ: Erlbaum.
Westbury, I. (1998). Didaktik and curriculum. In B. Gundem & S. Hopmann (Eds.) (1998). *Didaktik and/or curriculum: An international dialogue* (pp. 47–78-8). New York, NY: Peter Lang.
Westbury, I. (1995). Didaktik and curriculum theory: Are they the two sides of the same coin? In S. Hopmann & K. Riquarts (Eds.). *Didaktik and/or curriculum* (pp. 187–200). Kiel: Institut für die Pädagogik der Naturwissenschaften.
Westbury, I., Hopmann, S., & Riquarts, K. (Eds.) (2000). *Teaching as a reflective practice: The German Didaktik tradition*. Mahwah, NJ: Erlbaum.
Wolff-Metternich, B. S. von (2004). Was heißt heute: sich im Denken orientieren? In W. Frühwald, J. Limbach, A. Schavan, D. Schipanski, M. G. Schmidt, L. Schorn-Schütte, & B. S. von WolffMetternich (Eds.). *Sind wir noch ein Volk der Dichter und Denker?* (pp. 65–76). Heidelberg, Germany: Universitätsverlag Winter.

5 Conclusion
Cosmopolitanism in a Latin American Key

There were my doctoral studies that brought my Latin American body to leave *Latinoamérica* to deepen my knowledge of the Anglo-Saxon tradition of Curriculum Studies. As a result of that process, I attempt to reconceptualize that tradition by thinking Curriculum Studies as a complicated international conversation. Somehow this is a response to my own doctoral experience, which along with deepening my knowledge of the U.S. curriculum tradition, also sends me back to my own Latin American tradition. From that hybrid space, I ask myself about the possibility of building an academic field that is truly international or worldly. The only way I can conceive of such a field is as an academic intercultural dialogue among equals. This intercultural dialogue, as opposed to cultural monologue, does not deny the past but works it through—which is to say, to recognize, resist, and work on the surpassing of neocolonial dynamics still present in the production, circulation, and exchanges of knowledge inside and outside the field of Curriculum Studies. There is no true internationalization without decolonization. An international field today is a decolonizing field. This is the work that any intercultural dialogue across educational traditions has ahead. Only out of that work, can a worldwide field of education emerge. At least that is my hope. My *locus enunciantis* is *Latinoamericana*; but it has a cosmopolitan vocation. This cosmopolitan vocation is another affinity I notice in the traditions I have tried to put into conversation. This final chapter elaborates on a cosmopolitan project for the field of Curriculum Studies based on having written this work, including both the path that may be noted in this writing and the detours that showed me the vastness and richness of the landscapes in which I begin to walk.

I start by addressing two main words that have come out of this work of international conversation informed by intercultural dialogue. These words are "hybridity" and "cosmopolitanism." Then I advance the word "translation" as useful to think about intercultural dialogue. I add the word translation as an important tradition to be taken into consideration when thinking the field of Curriculum Studies as cosmopolitan. To conclude I return to my work, finishing with a reflection upon the pages

I have written. In Benjamin's words, I finish with a thinking that thinks my thinking in reflection.

Hybridity

> Hybridization is underway.
>
> (Pinar, 2013, p. 58)

Hybridity has been an important part of the thinking about the internationalization of Curriculum Studies (Autio, 2014; Casimiro Lopes & Macedo, 2014a, 2014b; Chambers. 2003; Díaz-Barriga, 2014; Díaz-Barriga & García-Garduño, 2014; García-Garduño, 2011; Miranda de Moraes, 2014; Montoya-Vargas, 2014; Moreira, 2003; Niculescu, Norel, & Usaci, 2014; Pinar, 2011, 2014a, 2014b; Vaish, 2014; Rivera, 2003). This is not just because the discourse of globalization proposes the idea of a society "beyond a narrative of closure, and constantly transgressing boundaries," for which, "as a parallel process, the self must define itself to another as a process of hybridity" (Autio, 2014, p. 29). Although the hybrid "that emerges takes its most expressive form in everyday life" (Pinar, 2014a, p. 522), it may be argued that hybridity has been a covered-up reality that the national imagination can no longer sustain. The concern for purity is mistaken when confronted by historical and geographical developments. In the second decade of the twenty-first century, hybridity emerged as a value for the field of curriculum becoming a worldwide-non-uniform educational field. In that process contemporary curriculum discourses "are now being reconceptualized into hybrid forms" (Pinar, 2014a, p. 522) as the internationalization of the conversation of Curriculum Studies gets underway.

> Curriculum discourses can also be studied as hybrid as they correspond to transitory configurations that result from different traditions and pedagogic movements. To understand these discourses, it is necessary to analyze them not only as results of dispute among conceptual currents, but also as manifestations of unresolved conflicts. Thus, the hybridization category can be considered especially useful for a study that focuses on the process in which distinct trends, models, and curriculum theories, both new and previously existent, are mobilized and articulated in a determined place, thereby creating, within possible limits, new meanings.
>
> (Moreira, 2003, p. 172)

In this same line of thought, Frida Díaz-Barriga (2014) has pointed out that processes of hybridity take place when "structures and practices that stem from diverse origins can combine in order to create new entities in a kind of crossbreeding process that is never free from contradictions and exclusions" (p. 329). These contradictions and exclusions, especially in the Global South, make the process of hybridity lead to "disjunctive syntheses" as "the coming together of disparate ideas" (p. 555), as Rivera (2003) has suggested.

These tensions are strong in *Latinoamérica*, where the field of Curriculum Studies coexists with the traditions of *Didáctica* and *Pedagogía*. In that sense, each other's critique regarding the other as an instrumental approach to education is a commonplace among them. Again, the landscapes are diverse across countries. Pedagogy is usually associated with more grassroots organizations and teacher movements, as Montoya-Vargas (2014) has shown in the Colombian context. On the other hand, in the Brazilian context, Alice Casimiro Lopes and Elizabeth Macedo (2014a) have pointed out "the difficulty of defining the boundaries of the field and from then on defended its hybrid character" (p. 86) in which the "incorporation of post-structuralist theoretical contributions in the curriculum field started through a hybrid process with critical perspectives" (p. 96) in an effort to overcome the "positivistic, fragmented, and alienated conception of science that dominated the school curriculum" (Miranda de Moraes, 2014, p. 101). Therefore, "we do not consider that this hybridity is a failure, a mistake, or even an evil to be overcome" (Casimiro Lopes & Macedo, 2014a, p. 97). On the contrary, as I have previously written, this hybridity is the result of a mindset that wanted to be *latinoamericano* while it remains open to intercultural dialogue. The Latin American field of curriculum had from the beginning this cosmopolitan vocation. At the end of the day, hybridity may be considered an intellectual analogue, perhaps a reconstruction, of *Latinoamérica*'s *mestizo* existential condition. What may have been praised as our weakness, may be today our strength.

Cosmopolitanism

> My Recifeness explained my Pernambucanity . . . the later clarified my Northeastness, which in turn shed light on my Brazilianity, my Brazilianity elucidated my Latin Americanness, and the later made me a person of the world.
>
> (Freire, 1994, p. 87)

Despite the increasing popularity of the word "cosmopolitanism" in thinking of internationalization, this is already problematic. That is, I think, its strength. It certainly has a historical past that connects it to Eurocentrism and imperialism but there are communities that reject those tendencies. According to Fazal Rizvi (2009), a sufficient account of cosmopolitanism must rely on the fact that "global connectivity has become a pervasive socio-cultural condition, and attempts to understand the dynamics of intercultural relations should no longer be aligned entirely to local and national requirements and prejudices, but should instead seek to become cosmopolitan" (p. 254). In fact, it is precisely that planetary experience that makes necessary intercultural dialogue and a cosmopolitan attitude to the *Otro*. Delanty (2009), on the other hand, has stated that "for cosmopolitanism, the significance resides in the notion of hybridity" (p. 65), a concept, that according to this author, has "wider resonance in cultural approaches to globalization," especially regarding the development of a hybrid culture emerging from transnational movement of "people and cultures" (p. 65). Hybrid cosmopolitanism requires persons to engage in conversation as equals in order to become something else while remaining somehow the same. This idea has generated hyphenated definitions of cosmopolitanism that attempt to show their suitability to respond to the planetary existence of humanity and the particularity of the experiences within which they live: what Appiah (2005) terms rooted cosmopolitanism. Harvey (2009) has described this in the following terms:

> Against this universal vision are ranged all manner of hyphenated versions of cosmopolitanism, variously described as "rooted," "situated," "actually existing," "discrepant," "vernacular," "Christian," "bourgeois," "liberal," "postcolonial," "feminist," "proletarian," "subaltern," "ecological," "socialist", and so forth. Cosmopolitanism here gets particularized and pluralized in the belief that detached loyalty to the abstract category of "the human" is incapable in theory, let alone in practice, of providing any kind of political purchase on the strong currents of globalization and international interventionism that swirl around us.
>
> (p. 79)

Therefore, he insists, cosmopolitanism "reemerged from the shadows and [has] shaken off many of its negative connotations," not just from its Eurocentric roots but also from those times when "Jews, communists, and cosmopolitans were cast as traitors to national solidarities and at best vilified and at worst sent to concentration camps" (Harvey, 2009, p. 78). Today this Southern cosmopolitanism arises out of the global opposition to neoliberal globalization and neo-imperialism.

In the field of education, and specifically in Curriculum Studies, globalization has developed a global curriculum through standardized testing. Haunted by this process, Pinar (2015b) claims that "the curriculum remains nationally based, locally enacted and individually experienced" (p. 235). These contexts have tendencies toward cosmopolitanism and provincialism, Pinar insists. Nevertheless, cosmopolitanism, as opposed to the provincialism which characterizes Eurocentric thinking (Galcerán Huget, 2016; Dussel, 2011, 1973a; Chakrabarty, 2000), remains still a project for the field of curriculum to combat the neocolonial dynamics at play today yet under a call for global education (Nussbaum, 1996).

As noted earlier, Pinar uses the word internationalization over globalization because the latter suggests a neocolonial or neo-imperialistic process.

More than 15 years after that moment, Pinar (2015a) said that "nothing could be more important now, it seems to me, than nationally distinctive fields engaging in sustained dialogue with each other, forging a 'new internationalism'" (p. 230). Therefore, he continues, the worldwide recontextualization of this field in "nations with distinctive histories and cultures will underline its [the field's] localized and reconstructed character. The particular remains primary despite globalization and its common denominator: standardization through assessment and technology" (Pinar, 2015a, p. 229). Nevertheless, this concern with globalization and choice of internationalization is not the only reason for which the word cosmopolitanism is more and more used to describe the project of internationalization in Curriculum Studies. Another concern is to take distance from the global discourse and its insistence on multiculturalism. This global discourse has been criticized for the emphasis upon identity that usually comprises. Pinar (2009) explains this concern in the following terms:

> [T]he centrality of identity in multiculturalism also poses dangers, among them a tendency to stereotype when summarizing ethnicities and other groups, as well as the splintering of the social, e.g., shared responsibilities and aspirations. The point of a cosmopolitan education, as Anderson (2006) reminds, is to achieve distance from such identities: "There is, of course, a term that throughout its long philosophical, aesthetic, and political history has been used to denote cultivated detachment from restrictive forms of identity, and that term is 'cosmopolitanism'" (p. 72). Anderson then emphasizes cosmopolitanism's "reflective distance from one's cultural affiliations."
>
> (p. 13)

In the line of thought we have been following, one could say that multiculturalism favors difference rather that distinctiveness while cosmopolitanism cultivates hybridity informed by distinctiveness. Dimitriadis and McCarthy argue in a similar way that "multicultural education . . . attempts to 'discipline' difference rather than be transformed by it" (quoted in Pinar, 2009, p. 2). This transformation is possible as long as an intercultural dialogue is possible. Multiculturalism is the acknowledgement of a situation: there are multicultural differences within and outside national borders. Therefore, if multiculturalism recognizes a situation historically denied by the national imagination and Eurocentric universalism, cosmopolitanism nurtured by intercultural dialogue is a step ahead.

This cosmopolitan vocation has been part of the Latin American thinking of liberation from its beginnings. The formulation of a philosophy of liberation was suggested by Dussel in the early 1970s as a new moment in the history of human philosophy, "an analogical moment that is born after European, Russian, and North American modernity, but anteceding African and Asian postmodern philosophy which alongside us constitutes the proximal worldly future: philosophy of poor peoples, philosophy of human-worldly liberation" (Dussel, 1973a, p. 173). This is, according to Dussel, a "barbarian philosophy," (p. 173) which emerges from the non-being of the provincial Europe and its confusion about its Europeanness with humanness. It is precisely because *Latinoamérica* is "beyond the European totality, modern and domineering, this philosophy of future is worldly, postmodern, and of liberation" (Dussel, 1973a, p. 174). Dussel (1973b) elaborates:

> Because it departs from the Other's revelation and it thinks his/her word, this analectical thinking is the Latin American philosophy, unique and new, the first truly postmodern and surpassing of Europeanness. Neither Schelling, nor Feuerbach, nor Marx, nor Kierkegaard nor Levinas could transcend Europe. We have been born outside; we have suffered it. Suddenly misery becomes richness! This is the authentic philosophy of misery that Proudhon had wanted to write.
> (p. 162)

It is intriguing that the use of the word "postmodern"[1] to refer to this world-wide philosophy comes after Eurocentric modernity. The usage of the term by Dussel precedes by almost a decade Lyotard's naming of the condition of advanced capitalism that we, from the underside of modernity, named late modernity. The obsession with difference in this postmodern thinking makes it provincial, arguing that difference makes communication impossible. On the contrary, the Latin American thinking stresses distinctiveness that does not prevent cultures from human understanding. That is the contribution made possible by this barbarian philosophy and its analectical pedagogy.

To me Dussel's concept of analectics and Benjamin's elective affinities may contribute to forward an intercultural dialogue across educational traditions. That is what I have suggested in the constellations pointed to in the previous chapter and more generally within this study. Having that in mind, I will suggest now that this intercultural dialogue may be developed by focusing on specific words that the international conversation in the field of curriculum has used to name its worldwide dimensions. Since these words belong to diverse educational traditions that exist in different languages, I believe that translation can provide insights to advance such a task. Translation is necessarily intercultural and concerned with communication among languages. Therefore, it appears to me suitable to think that authentic international involvement in an academic field requires that the same terms used in its study become objects of that study (Pinar, 2006). In the next part of this final chapter, I advance some ideas that elaborate on this suggestion. I address the topic and process of translation as helpful to think about the intercultural dialogue in which Curriculum Studies as an international conversation requires us to engage.

Translation

During the last decades, translation no longer refers to just written linguistic translation but to any endeavor that entails conveying meaning from one domain to another. In that way, translation has become a field usually called upon in current conversations in philosophy, cultural studies, political theory, and so on. Situated in the field of Translation Studies, Bermann and Porter (2014) argue that translation "has most often done its work in the shadows of official history. But it has begun to grow in visibility with the globalizing culture of the twentieth and twenty-first centuries" (p. 1). There has been also a distrust of translated materials; its main expression has been the advice of reading in the language in which the text was written, particularly when it comes to philosophical texts. The saying *tradutotere tradittore* summarizes that distrust, pointing to a tension between fidelity and treason.

> As translator she mediates between antagonistic cultural and historical domains. If we assume that language is always in some sense metaphoric, then, any discourse, oral or written, is liable to be implicated in treachery when perceived to be going beyond repetition of what the community perceives as the "true" and/or "authentic" concept, image, or narrative. The act of translating, which often introduces different concepts and perceptions, displaces and may even do violence to local knowledge through language. In the process, these may be assessed as false or inauthentic.
> (Alarcón, 2003, p. 35)

For various reasons, the status of translation today is discussed in such a sophisticated manner. In his influential work *The Experience of the Foreign*, Berman (1992) has affirmed:

> The very aim of translation—to open up in writing a certain relation with the Other, to fertilize what is one's Own thought through the mediation of what is foreign—is diametrically opposed to the ethnocentric structure of every culture, that species of narcissism by which every society must remain a pure and adulterated whole.
> (p. 4)

The essence of translation, Berman continues, is "to be an opening, a dialogue, a crossbreeding, a decentering. Translation is 'a putting in touch with, or it is *nothing*'" (p. 4). Therefore, in spite of the hardship of "dialogue between cultures ... that cannot be separated from their roots on languages" (Kemp, 2011, p. 67), this faith in communicability across languages has its correspondence in what is called the approximating character of translation. Drawing on Benjamin (1968), Berman emphasizes the affirmative character of translation which makes it work "against Babel, against the reign of difference, against the empirical" (p. 7). This affirmative character of translation is what makes it so appealing when thinking of intercultural dialogue.

In his book *Epistemologies from the South* (2014), De Sousa Santos draws upon Gramsci's concept of "living philology" to develop an understanding of intercultural translation as "a living process of complex interactions among heterogeneous artifacts" (p. 338). His definition sounds quite appealing for a project like mine, having intellectual history as a main component. Besides this, De Sousa Santos sounds very cosmopolitan when claiming that the emphasis on the possibility of intercultural communication in "translation undermines the idea of original or pure cultures and stresses the idea of cultural rationality" (p. 341). The Portuguese author understands the work of translation to be a collective as well as a political task. It seems that translation is not only a good mode to think about intercultural dialogue, but it is a way of doing intercultural dialogue itself. The work of translation, De Sousa Santos writes, supposes "a nonconformist attitude vis-à-vis the limits of one's knowledge and practice and the readiness to be surprised and to learn with and from the *Otro*'s knowledge and practice in order to build collaborative actions of mutual advantage" (p. 354). This is where a cosmopolitan, ergo intercultural, ergo decolonizing, scholarship resides. I think of the project of spaces for cultivating cosmopolitan scholarship, ergo intercultural, ergo decolonizing, as an academic intercultural dialogue focused on intercultural translation of educational concepts. It is a collective study of concepts decontextualized in a plurality of cultural geographies.

The idea of translation helps here to understand that there is no reproduction of the same but a new understanding in which something remains while it has become something else. As Benjamin remarks in *The Task of the Translator* (Benjamin, 1968), the task of translation "consists in finding that intended effect upon the language into which he is translating which produces in it the echo of the original" (p. 75). It is an echo that comes from the attentiveness of listening rather than the certainty of seeing. Sandra Bermann (2005) points out that this is Benjamin's reminder that "such translation is a temporal as well as a geo-linguistic or spatial affair" (p. 269). The translator, she continues "elicits the echo not only of a different but also of a previous language in his or her own" (p. 269). It is the creating of an elective affinity between the original text and the new text. Elective affinities are not identical but analogical.

I would like to suggest another step forward and to propose that a space for cosmopolitan educational scholarship, ergo intercultural, ergo decolonizing, can be reached by focusing on the translation of the untranslatable. By untranslatable I mean the words existing in every language that cannot be easily translated into another language, words that cannot be translated into one other word but that require explanation. Those are the words that trigger conversation. They force those wanting to understand within the intercultural dialogue to address "the question, what do you mean by that?" In his introduction to the English version of the *Dictionary of Untranslatables: A Philosophical Lexicon* (Cassin, Apter, Lezra, & Wood, 2014), Wood writes:

> To speak of *untranslatables* in no way implies that the terms in question, or the expressions, the syntactical or grammatical turns, are not and cannot be translated: the untranslatable is rather what one keeps on (not) translating. But this indicates that their translation, into one language or another, creates a problem, to the extent of sometimes generating a neologism or imposing a new meaning on an old word. It is a sign of the way in which, from one language to another, neither the words nor the conceptual networks can simply be superimposed.
> (p. xvii)

Confronted by the impossibility of a ready-made response, the one wanting to understand must wait for the *Otro* to be revealed through his words, while the one wanting to be understood must multiply his or her effort to echo the old that must remain in the new. In other words, they must engage in a work of elective affinity. An example of such untranslatable words, as we had already pointed out in this work, is the German word *Bildung*. Its intrinsic elusiveness makes it untranslatable (Horlacher, 2017; Autio, 2014; Pinar, 2011; Løvlie & Standish, 2002; Gundem & Hopmann, 1998). *Bildung* has no equivalent neither in English nor in Spanish. Some common translations are education, culture, formation, self-cultivation. The *Dictionary of Untranslatables* includes *Bildung* as an "untranslatable;" "the term Bildung is certainly one of those words whose translation seems the most aleatory," (Cassin et al., 2014, p. 111). This is not just an anecdotal allusion as it might seem, but a confirmation that the untranslatability of the word *Bildung* is addressed by translation experts as well as by educational thinkers. As such, conversations around it have been present in several intellectual projects of international scholarship in education enriching our language in the formation of a worldwide non-uniformed field of Curriculum Studies, as a language in between (Aoki, 2005), as if in this case also

> the expression "formation (*Bildung*) of the language" is almost a motto that is today on almost everyone's lips: writers, art critics, translators, scientists. Each of them wants to form (bilden) it in his own way: and one is often opposed to the other. What should we do

if everyone is allowed to form (*bilden*) it: shall I then be authorized to ask what "form" (bilden) means? What is a language without formation (ungebildete Sprache)? And what revolutions have other languages undergone before they appeared formed (ausgebildet)?[2]

In addressing the translation of the untranslatable, *Bildung* with all its "problems of intercultural communications" (Gundem & Hopmann, 1998, p. 1) may keep triggering complicated conversations.

The Beginning of the Afterlife

> The critic's task is complicated and often thankless. He must learn the language of the language in order to make intelligible his criticism. Such learning nearly always occurs because the critic has come to age in the heritage. It is usually through his own painful conflict that he comes to see the inadequacies of the taken-for-granted.
> (Pinar, 2015b, p. 35)

I address what has just been written in order to become aware of what I have done. My final words are concerned with the afterlife of this text. This idea of the afterlife of texts is tied to Benjamin's concept of criticism. He grounded his understanding of criticism in his study of German romanticism, which led him to define criticism as thinking that thinks its thinking in reflection. Therefore, what has been thought has to be rethought reflexively. In its performance, criticism keeps the text alive; it rejuvenates it. The work of intellectual bio-history that has become central to this study, a variant of the regressive-progressive and analytical-synthetical method of *currere*, has this concept of criticism at its center. The theoretical *détente* in Chapter 2 provided the space to release tension among intellectual traditions, within and without the field of education, enabling ideas to converse around words. Becoming the gravitational center of vivid constellations, those words helped me to try a way of holding together a force field that became the theoretical possibility of across-traditions constellations. As a consequence, this exercise advanced the idea of understanding curriculum as an international conversation, a constellation gravitating around the word curriculum, among scholars that belong to and move across distinctive educational traditions. This is consistent with the understanding of curriculum as a divergent field naming itself as such in a plurality of contexts unevenly connected. This experience of addressing polysemy may also help the field to go beyond itself into an intercultural conversation to which analogical thinking may contribute. These thoughts are also grounded in the cosmopolitan *Experiencia Latinoamericana* [Latin American experience] where the analectical pedagogy of a philosophy-theology of liberation invites us to lived polysemy not just in the relation word-eye but also and urgently in the relation word-ear.

Paired together, the first two moments of the method of *currere* opened a space in which resonances suggest a dialectical relation between the 1960s and the 1990s, between regressive and progressive moments in history, between the biographical, scholarly, and historical "givens" and the interpellation of the *Otro*, including the generational *Otro*. The neocolonial arrival of field of curriculum in the 1960s was put into tension with the Latin American educational tradition whose major figures began the critique of schooling in the underside of modernity. A truly intercultural intellectual dialogue took place at that time among Latin American and U.S. thinkers whose dimension and depth are still to be studied. The *Otro* emerged in the 1990s, the peoples of *Abya-Yala*, rejecting the celebration of the Fifth Centenary and resonating with the Latin American thinkers of liberation and the *Pedagógica Latinoaméricana*, born by listening to their interpellation. Therefore, *Latinoamérica* is acknowledged as a dual, hybrid, *mestizo* continent born from the invasion of this land and the domination of its peoples by Europe. That is why the *mestizo latinoamericano* is the dialectical image of modernity. Modernity is to be thought as modernity-coloniality in affinity with its historical process of constitution. The critique of this dialectical image enables the critique of the narrative of modernity and a reconstructive intercultural dialogue.

The critique of the intellectual history of the academic field of Curriculum Studies has been reread from the perspective of the possibility of building a worldwide academic field based on intercultural dialogue across traditions. This movement is performed by the *analytical-synthetical*. The main focus, of course, has been the relations between the United States and *Latinoamérica* deployed upon the field of education and specifically upon two educational traditions within that field. I have tried to do so, being aware that for those living in the Global South, a necessary epistemological vigilance is always required when our intellectual curiosity takes us to study the intellectual production of the world-system's center. This curiosity cannot lead us to a critical imitation of it but to engage in dialogue with it. We must read writing. That is a central problematic for the *analéctica pedagógica* as "the human mode to address tradition" (Dussel, 1973a, p. 131). That has been my intention in joining an international conversation begun some time ago, maybe before becoming aware of it. I have explored these different educational traditions looking for correspondences rather than the dissonances. In that endeavor, I found not just the conceptual resonances reported herein, but also a methodological approach to address that task. This is the task of cultural criticism, to look for the critical potential of every culture, listening for resonances in sometimes long-forgotten texts, sometimes through not yet performed readings. To me, the building of that planetary differential consciousness is a matter of both historical-personal reconstruction and of human survival.

Looking to make sense of my educational doctoral experience, I have become aware of my understanding of academic life, the idea of a life in study. This is a life devoted to the study of a discipline—a life consecrated to the study of cultural contents organized in collections of knowledge we name variously subject matters, academic fields, academic disciplines, etc. To say a consecrated life is to say a life in a profession. At the center of this life, in my case, has been study of the complex and elusive relation between the personal and the collective, the biographical and the historical, the critique of the present and the work of imagination. Certainly, it is a work of elective affinity and much work waiting to be done. I have attempted to address that work, focusing on the understanding of Curriculum Studies as an international conversation. This work solves no problem but it does pose many.

Notes

1. In his book *The Idea of Postmodernism: A History* (2005), Hans Bertens affirms: "Since Michael Köhler published his '"Postmodernismus": einbegriffsgeschichtlicher Überblick' in 1977, a wide range of early uses of the terms postmodern and postmodernism has come to light. Wolfgang Welsch tells us that 'postmodern' was used as early as the 1870s (Welsch, 1987, p. 12) and 'postmodernism' made its first appearance in the title of a book in 1926. 'Postmodern' resurfaced in 1934, in 1939, and in the 1940s. From then on sightings begin to multiply. There is, however, very little continuity between these early uses and the debate on postmodernism as it gets underway in the course of the 1960s" (p. 19).
2. Quote by Heder in (Cassin et al., 2014, p. 113).

References

Alarcón, N. (2003). Traddutora, Traditora: A paradigmatic figure of Chicana feminism. In M. C. Gutmann, F. V. Matos Rodríguez, L. Stephen, & P. Zavella (Eds.). *Perspectives on Las Americas: A reader in culture, history and representation* (pp. 33–49). Maldem, MA: Blackwell Publishers.
Aoki, T. (2005). *Curriculum in a new key: The collected works of Ted T. Aoki*. Mahwah, NJ: Lawrence Erlbaum Associates.
Appiah, K. A. (2005). *"The ethics of identity": A rooted cosmopolitism*. Princeton, NJ: Princeton University Press
Autio. T. (2014). The internationalization of curriculum research. In W. F. Pinar (Ed.) *International handbook of curriculum research* (2nd ed., pp. 17–31). Mahwah, NJ: Lawrence Erlbaum Associates.
Benjamin, W. (1968). *Illuminations*. New York, NY: Schocken Books.
Berman, A. (1992). *The experience of the foreign: Culture and translation in romantic Germany*. Albany, NY: State University of New York Press.
Bermann, S. (2005). Translating history. In S. Bermann & M. Wood (Eds.). *Nation, language, and the ethics of translation* (pp. 257–273). Princeton, NJ: Princeton University Press.
Bermann, S., & Porter, C. (Eds.) (2014). *A companion to translation studies*. Hoboken, NJ: Wiley-Blackwell.
Bertens, H. (2005). *The idea of postmodernism: A history*. New York, NY: Routledge.

Casimiro Lopes, A., & Macedo, E. (2014a). The curriculum field in Brazil since the 1990s. In W. F. Pinar (Ed.). *International handbook of curriculum research* (2nd ed., pp. 86–100). Mahwah, NJ: Lawrence Erlbaum Associates.

Casimiro Lopes, A., & Macedo, E. (2014b). Movimientos recientes en el campo del curriculum en Brasil: articulaciones entre las perspectivas postestructurales y marxistas. In A. Diaz Barriga & J. M. Garcia-Garduño (Eds.). *Desarrollo del Curriculum en América Latina: Experiencia de diez países* (pp. 89–104). Buenos Aires: Miño y Dávila.

Cassin, B., Apter, E., Lezra, J., & Wood, M. (Eds.) (2014). *Dictionary of untranslatables: A philosophical lexicon.* Princeton, NJ: Princeton University Press.

Chakrabarty, D. (2000). *Provincializing Europe: Postcolonial thought and historical difference.* Princeton, NJ: Princeton University Press.

Chambers, C. (2003). "As Canadian as possible under the circumstances": A view of contemporary curriculum discourses in Canada. In W. F. Pinar (Ed.). *Handbook of research on curriculum* (1st ed., pp. 221–232). Mahwah, NJ: Lawrence Erlbaum Associates.

Delanty, G. (2009). *The cosmopolitan imagination: The renewal of critical social theory.* Cambridge: Cambridge University Press.

De Sousa Santos, B. (2014). *Epistemologies of the South: Justice against epistemicide.* London: Routledge.

Díaz-Barriga, F. (2014). Curriculum research in Mexico. In W. F. Pinar (Ed.). *Handbook of research on curriculum* (2nd ed., pp. 329–339). Mahwah, NJ: Lawrence Erlbaum Associates.

Díaz-Barriga, A., & García-Garduño, J. M. (2014). *Desarrollo del curriculum en América Latina: Experiencia de diez países.* Buenos Aires: Miño y Dávila editores.

Dussel, E. (2011). *Politics of liberation: A critical world history.* London: SCM Press.

Dussel, E. (1973a). *Para una ética de la liberación latinoamericana.* Buenos Aires: Siglo Veintiuno Argentina Editores. V1.

Dussel, E. (1973b). *Para una ética de la liberación latinoamericana.* Buenos Aires: Siglo Veintiuno Argentina Editores. V2.

Freire, P. (1994). *Pedagogy of hope: Reliving pedagogy of the oppressed.* New York, NY: Continuum.

Galcerán Huget, M. (2016). *La bárbara Europa: Una mirada desde el postcolonialismo y la decolonialidad.* Madrid: Traficantes de Sueños.

García-Garduño, J. M. (2011). The institutionalization of curriculum studies in Mexico: Understanding acculturation, hybridity, cosmopolitanism in Ibero-American curriculum studies. In W. F. Pinar (Ed.). *Curriculum studies in Mexico: Intellectual histories, present circumstances* (pp. 137–164). New York, NY: Palgrave Macmillan.

Gundem, B., & Hopmann, S. (1998). Introduction: Didaktik meets curriculum. In B. Gundem & S. Hopmann (Eds.) (1998). *Didaktik and/or curriculum: An international dialogue* (pp. 1–8). New York, NY: Peter Lang.

Harvey, D. (2009). *Cosmopolitanism and the geographies of freedom.* New York, NY: Columbia University Press.

Horlacher, R. (2017). *The educated subject and the German concept of Bildung: A comparative cultural history.* New York, NY: Routledge.

Kemp, P. (2011). *Citizen of the world: The cosmopolitan ideal for the twenty-first century.* Amherst, NY: Humanities Books.

Løvlie, L., & Standish, P. (2002). Introduction: Bildung and the idea of a liberal education. *Journal of Philosophy of Education, 36*(3), 317–340.

Miranda de Moraes, S. E. (2014). Curriculum tendencies in Brazil. In W. F. Pinar (Ed.). *International handbook of curriculum research* (2nd ed., pp. 101–111). Mahwah, NJ: Lawrence Erlbaum Associates.

Montoya-Vargas, J. (2014). Curriculum studies in Colombia. In W. F. Pinar (Ed.). *International handbook of curriculum research* (2nd ed., pp. 134–150). Mahwah, NJ: Lawrence Erlbaum Associates.

Moreira, A. (2003). The curriculum field in Brazil: Emergence and consolidation. In W. F. Pinar (Ed.). *Handbook of research on curriculum* (1st ed., pp. 171–182). Mahwah, NJ: Lawrence Erlbaum Associates.

Niculescu, R. M., Norel, M., & Usaci, D. (2014). Curriculum: A constant concern in Romania. In W. F. Pinar (Ed.). *International handbook of curriculum research* (2nd ed., pp. 411–426). Mahwah, NJ: Lawrence Erlbaum Associates.

Nussbaum, M. (1996). Patriotism and cosmopolitanism. In J. Cohen (Ed.). *For love of country: Debating the limits of patriotism*. Chicago: University of Chicago Press.

Pinar, W. F. (2015a). *Educational experience as lived: Knowledge, history, alterity*. New York, NY: Palgrave Macmillan.

Pinar, W. F. (2015b). Self and others. In W. F. Pinar & M. R. Grumet. *Toward a poor curriculum* (pp. 8–39). Kingston, NY: Educator's International Press.

Pinar, W. F. (2014a). Curriculum research in the United States: Crisis, reconceptualization, internationalization. In W. F. Pinar (Ed.). *International handbook of curriculum research* (2nd ed., pp. 521–532). Mahwah, NJ: Lawrence Erlbaum Associates.

Pinar, W. F. (Ed.) (2014b). *International handbook of curriculum research*. Mahwah, NJ: Lawrence Erlbaum Associates.

Pinar, W. F. (2013). *Curriculum studies in the United States: Present circumstances, intellectual histories*. Houndmills, NH: Palgrave Macmillan.

Pinar, W. F. (2011). *The character of curriculum studies: Bildung, currere, and the recurring question of the subject*. New York, NY: Palgrave Macmillan.

Pinar, W. F. (2009). *The worldliness of a cosmopolitan education passionate lives in public service*. New York, NY: Routledge.

Pinar, W. F. (2006). *The synoptic text today and other essays: Curriculum development after the reconceptualization*. New York, NY: Peter Lang.

Rivera, F. D. (2003). In Southeast Asia: Philippines, Malaysia, and Thailand: Conjunctions and collisions in the global cultural economy. In W. F. Pinar (Ed.). *Handbook of research on curriculum* (1st ed., pp. 553–574). Mahwah, NJ: Lawrence Erlbaum Associates.

Rizvi, F. (2009). Towards cosmopolitan learning. *Discourse: Studies in the Cultural Politics of Education, 30*(3), 253–268.

Vaish, V. (2014). Curriculum in Singapore. In W. F. Pinar (Ed.). *International handbook of curriculum research* (2nd ed., pp. 439–444). Mahwah, NJ: Lawrence Erlbaum Associates.

Index

acculturation 7, 61
Adorno, T. W. 28, 101–102
analectical 6, 88, 94, 95, 97, 121, 125
analogy 30, 37, 78, 92–94, 107
analytical 14, 15, 17–19, 29, 37, 38, 45, 77–79, 82, 85, 92, 93, 125, 126
Appel, M. 3, 104, 106, 109
Autio, T. 4, 10, 98–102, 107, 108, 117, 124
autoethnography 11, 17

Benjamin, W. 14, 16, 28, 31, 36, 44–46, 52, 93–95, 117, 121, 123, 125
Berman, A. 122, 123
Bermann, S. 122, 123
Bilbao, F. 33, 34
Bildung 93, 98, 100–105, 108, 109, 124, 125

conscientização 38, 58, 72
conversation 1–5, 7, 8, 11, 13–21, 29, 30, 31, 32, 33, 35, 36, 41, 43, 44, 54, 58, 60, 65, 71, 72, 78, 81, 83, 95, 98, 103, 105, 106, 116, 117, 119, 121, 122, 124, 125, 126, 127
cosmopolitanism 10, 15, 19, 87, 93, 116, 118, 119, 120
cultural monologue 6, 30, 32, 66, 116
culture of silence 31, 41, 47, 48, 50, 53–58, 60, 66, 67, 68
currere 11–15, 17–21, 36, 58, 92, 93, 95, 98, 100, 102, 103, 125, 126
Curriculum History 82
Curriculum Studies 1–11, 13–20, 26, 28, 44, 49, 50, 52, 58, 71, 78–84, 86, 87, 89, 93, 95–104, 106–109, 116–120, 122, 124, 126, 127
Curriculum Theory 15, 17, 19, 21, 58, 78, 82, 98, 99, 108

De Alba, A. 9, 10, 49
Denzin, N. 1, 11, 14, 16–17, 44, 73
De Sousa Santos, B. 6, 38, 123
dialogue 1, 2, 5, 6, 16, 17, 19, 30, 32, 37, 54–56, 60, 62, 63, 65, 67, 79, 84, 94, 97, 103, 107, 108, 116, 118–124, 126
Díaz-Barriga, A. 7, 8, 9, 10, 20, 49, 61, 117
Didaktik 19, 98–102, 104, 105, 108, 109
Dussel, E. 1, 6, 8, 15–16, 20, 26, 32–34, 46, 48, 55–57, 60, 62–68, 72, 78, 87–92, 94, 96, 97, 100, 119–121, 126

elective affinities 16, 78, 93–95, 107, 121, 123
Eurocentrism 38, 44, 56, 63, 64, 87, 118
existentialism 11, 71, 95, 103, 109
experience 1, 2, 10, 11, 12–13, 14–15, 19–21, 27, 32, 37, 41, 43, 44, 49, 50, 54, 56, 62, 70, 72, 77, 97, 100–103, 105, 108, 109, 116, 119, 122, 125, 126
exteriority 64, 67, 68, 72, 90, 91, 92, 94, 96, 97

Fanon, F. 2, 39, 48
force field 15, 18, 26–28, 36, 37, 44, 46, 106, 125
Frankfurt School 101
Freire, P. 2, 3, 7–9, 11–12, 15, 16, 20, 31, 32, 34, 35, 42, 43, 45, 47, 48, 50, 54–58, 62, 66, 67, 69, 70–72, 87, 92, 94, 95, 97, 98, 107, 118
Fromm, E. 35

Index

García-Garduño, J. M. 7–10, 20, 49, 52, 61, 117
Global South 6, 37, 38, 58, 64, 118, 126
González Camarena, J. 47
Greene, M. 7, 8, 58
Grumet, M. 4, 7, 8, 13, 14, 15, 73, 103

Halbbildung 101
Hegel, W. F. 33, 34, 57, 96
historical consciousness 12, 42, 96
history 6, 11, 12, 14–21, 29, 34, 36, 37, 41–46, 48–53, 60, 62, 68, 69, 70, 71, 77, 79, 80–85, 87, 88, 91, 92, 95, 97, 99, 101, 105, 109, 120, 121, 122, 123, 125, 126, 127
Horkheimer, M. 66, 96
Horlacher, R. 100, 104, 105, 108, 124
hybridity 8, 9, 19, 107, 116, 117–120

intercultural dialogue 1, 6, 17, 30, 32, 37, 60, 65, 79, 94, 97, 107, 108, 116, 118–124, 126
internationalization 1, 4–10, 17–19, 39, 58, 80–83, 86, 96, 98, 108, 116–120

Jay, M. 28, 36, 37, 44, 79
Johnson-Mardones, D. 7, 20, 42, 43, 69, 71, 108, 109, 110

Klafki, W. 98, 99, 102, 105
Kliebard, H. 17, 109

Latin American thinkers of liberation 2, 66, 126
Latinoamérica 1, 2, 6–10, 16, 18, 19, 29, 32–35, 38, 43, 44, 47, 49–51, 53, 55–63, 66–68, 88, 89, 107, 116, 118, 121, 126
Levinas, E. 64, 67, 68, 72, 92, 94, 96, 121
Leyton, M. 52, 53
liberation theology 3, 19, 60, 62, 69
liminal 1, 6, 13, 19, 68, 90
Lopes, A. C. 10, 117, 118
Löwy, M. 93, 94

Macedo, E. 10, 117, 118
Malinche 47, 60, 65, 91
Mapuche 33, 59, 61, 62, 72
Marxism 36
McCarthy, C. 3, 16, 38, 71, 85, 120
mestizo latinoamericano 44–48, 60, 65, 89, 126

method 11, 14–17, 21, 29, 36, 87, 91, 103, 125, 126
Mexican muralism 47
Miller, J. 9, 28
modernity 1, 2, 32, 33, 36, 43–48, 50, 58, 60, 62–66, 72, 87–91, 98, 100, 102, 107, 108, 121, 126

neocolonial 2, 4, 6, 7, 63, 89, 90, 116, 119, 120, 126
neo-imperialistic 4, 19, 120

Otro 2, 18, 19, 30–32, 34, 54, 56, 59, 60, 62–68, 88, 89, 91, 92, 98, 119, 123, 124, 126

Paz, O. 47
Pedagógica Latinoamericana 16, 58, 62, 66–68, 78, 79, 87–93, 95–98, 126
pedagogy 7, 8, 20, 31, 34, 35, 47, 48, 57, 58, 66, 67, 68, 70, 87, 89, 90, 91, 92, 97, 98, 105, 108, 109, 118, 121, 125
pedagogy of listening 31, 66–67, 92
pedagogy of silence 92
Pedagogy of the Oppressed (Freire) 20, 42, 57, 58, 67, 70–72
philosophy of liberation 16, 20, 34, 68, 87, 88, 96, 120
Pinar, W. F. 1, 4–13, 15, 16, 19, 20, 21, 28, 30, 32, 36, 41, 50, 58, 60, 72, 79, 80, 81, 82, 83, 84, 85, 86, 87, 95, 96, 97, 98, 101, 102, 103, 104, 105, 108, 109, 117, 119, 120, 121, 124, 125
Popkewitz, T. 4
postmodern 43, 85, 121, 127
progressive 11, 14, 15, 17–18, 29, 35–37, 41, 44, 59–60, 68, 102, 103, 125, 126
psychoanalysis 11, 35, 36, 95, 102, 103, 109

Quijano, A. 46

racism 63
reconceptualization 1, 3, 5–9, 20, 58, 60, 71, 72, 79–82, 84, 85, 87, 88, 95, 98, 100, 109
regressive 11, 14, 15, 17–18, 29, 35–37, 41, 44, 48, 49, 53, 60, 62, 68, 103, 125, 126

Sartre, J. P. 2, 11, 14, 28, 36, 37, 44, 71, 96

Schelling, J. 96, 97, 121
silence 30–32, 38, 41, 47, 48, 50, 53, 54, 56–58, 60, 66–68, 70, 72, 91, 95

theoretical *détente* 18, 26, 27, 38, 125
totality 66, 92, 94, 96, 97, 121
translation 8, 19, 20, 39, 77, 102, 116, 121–125

Tröhler, D. 4, 101
Tyler, R. 3, 7, 8, 20, 52, 53, 80, 85, 87, 100, 109

Wallerstein, I. 2, 63
Westbury, I. 4, 98, 100

Zea, L. 33, 34